The Woman Director

The Adventures of A Really Independent Filmmaker, Ages 6-36

Jürgen Vsych

(pronounced Yurgen Vy-zick)

with illustrations by Frank C. Papé from the book
Jurgen, A Comedy of Justice
and some rather bad illustrations by the author

Wroughten Books
WASHINGTON, D.C. • TORONTO • GLASGOW

Thanks Mom,
Thanks Grandmother,
Thanks Great-Grandmother,
Thanks Great-Great Grandmother,
etc.

First printing 2005

ISBN 0-9749879-0-5
LCCN 2003097115

ATTENTION CORPORATIONS, UNIVERSITIES, COLLEGES, AND PRO-FESSIONAL ORGANIZATIONS: Quantity discounts are available on bulk purchases of this book for educational, gift purposes, or as premiums for increasing magazine subscriptions or renewals. Special books or book excerpts can also be created to fit specific needs. For information, please contact Wroughten Books. www.TheWoman Director.com.

Table of Contents

Thanks!

Max von Sydow, Retna, Monty Python, Cricket
Peters, Frank C. Papé (who probably thought he was
doing illustrations for another book), all my poor
(and I mean, *poor*) casts and crews, Leonard Nimoy,
Leon Lederman, Gemma Jones, Sandra Johnson,
Janus Films, Katharine Hepburn, Bo-Erik Gyberg,
Allan Grant, Terry Gilliam and Amy Gilliam, Gra-
ham Chapman, Jeanne Casarotto, James Branch
Cabell (biographer of another *Jurgen)*, Sandra Ar-
cher and the librarians and security guards at the
Academy of Motion Picture Arts & Sciences Library,
and Ray Bradbury (and Tigger, too!).

List of Illustrations

Really good illustrations by Frank C. Papé from the book *Jurgen* by James Branch Cabell

Really bad illustrations by Jürgen Vsych

Cover photo by Cricket Peters

Back cover: Buster Keaton in *The Electric House*

The young Woman Director on the phone to the lab, photo by Dad

Groucho Marx as Captain Spaulding in the 1928 Broadway production of *Animal Crackers*, courtesy The Billy Rose Theatre Collection. . .

. . . Field Marshal Erwin Rommel in Africa, around 1943 (so *he* was imitating *Groucho*!)

Stabbed in the eye with purple tempera, photo by Mom

The disgusted Woman Director at Christmas, photo by Dad

Basil Rathbone, Boris Karloff, Peter Lorre and Vincent Price in *Lunch Break* 1962, photo by Allan Grant, © Time-Life Pictures/Getty Images

Jacob and Wilhelm Grimm. Oil portrait by Elisabeth Jerichau-Baumann, 1855.

Graham Chapman as Raymond Luxury Yacht, courtesy Monty Python

Ray Bradbury and Tigger, photo by Thomas Victor, courtesy Ray Bradbury

Bride of Frankenstein makeup test, photo by Jürgen Vsych

Terry Gilliam as *A Man with a Stoat through his Head*, courtesy Monty Python

Jürgen the Easter Bunny, photo by Mom

Ingmar Bergman directing *Cries and Whispers*, photo by Bo-Erik Gyberg © Retna/Camerapress

Max von Sydow, photo by Sandra Johnson © Retna Ltd.

Erich von Stroheim & Pierre Fresnay in *La Grande Illusion*, courtesy Janus Films

Katharine Hepburn in 1936, courtesy Katharine Hepburn

Method Director, photo by Ros Casselle

Ros Casselle and Sandy Black, my *Method Crew* for *Pay Your Rent, Beethoven*, photo by Jürgen Vsych

John Vickery and Patrick Todd in *$on for Sail*, photo by Jürgen Vsych

John Sayles at 2002 Cannes Film Festival, photo by Jürgen Vsych

Buster Keaton as The Dane in *Daydreams*

Lilian Baylis, photo by Gordon Anthony, courtesy the V&A Picture Library

Julia Lee in *Ophelia Learns to Swim*, photo by Bruce Coughran

Lauren Birkell in *Ophelia Learns to Swim*, photo by Jürgen Vsych

Leonard Nimoy and anonymous friend from the play *Visit to a Small Planet*, Pheasant Run Playhouse, Chicago, Illinois 1968, courtesy Leonard Nimoy

Dennis Price, Alec Guinness and Gordon Jackson; pipers Keith Faulkner and John Fraser in *Tunes of Glory*, courtesy Janus Films

Me and Guy Green at Mr. Green's Big 9-0 (November 5, 2003) photo taken by a nice lady with short blonde hair © Jürgen Vsych

The Desert Piper at Vasquez Rocks (aka Planet *Star Trek*), photo by Cricket Peters

Michelle Kwan performs *Scheherazade* at the 2002 U.S. Nationals © Leah Adams

Director Barbie directs some ham, photo by Jürgen Vsych

Author's Note

I started writing a diary at age 14, after reading *Anne Frank's Diary.* To avoid having my diary torched by my un-Otto Frankish father, I wrote in the lines of my music homework notebooks, and created my own language—sort of a German-English-Japanese concoction blended with Chico Marx ice cream Italian, music notes representing letters, and some Egyptian hieroglyphics.

Despite precautions, in 1983, all my diaries, plays, screenplays and films were destroyed in a fire (in a fireplace, on a hot summer's day, to be precise). Events beginning from birth were re-recorded in subsequent diaries to the best of my 16-year-old memory (calendars, letters, photos, household receipts and back issues of the *Los Angeles Times* also provided clues). From June 2002 to January 2003, I read (for the first time) all 17,256 pages of my diaries. Ninety-five percent of my diaries' entries relate to directing, but that would make this book longer than *Pepys's Diaries.*

My diaries were written in a style meant solely to jog my memory, to remind me what I was feeling and thinking at the time, not in eloquent prose to be read by another pair of eyes. Therefore, instead of simply editing those 17,256 pages, I wrote this book in the present tense in order to put my brain right smack in the moment. This is also an excellent excuse for the poor grammar in the early chapters. Whenever possible, vocabulary and slang have been left intact; some archaic Angeleno adjectives have been translated into English. Most of the names have been changed, although the names of in/famous people are real.

Jürgen Vsych, Los Angeles
November 2003

CHAPTER 1

November 1973, Age 6

Wroughten Films

MGM

Michael, the brattiest kid in my kindergarten class, shows off his dad on Parents' Day. Michael's dad works at MGM (*M*etro-*G*oldwyn-*M*ayer, the movie studio across the street from Vets Park in Culver City. Vets Park isn't named for veterinarians—it's named for veter*ans* [men who fought in wars and now have nothing to do, so the government gave them a park to play chess in]. A war just ended [did we win? We're still speaking English, but there were no ticker tape parades, and when I ask about it, everyone changes the subject]).

. . . what was I talking about?. . . oh yeah—Michael's dad brought us film! He got it out of MGM's trash can (they were just going to throw it away!). It's 35mm—a lot bigger than the Super-8 film my Dad's camera uses. We have a projector at home, and show our home movies on the livingroom wall. We close the curtains so we can see it better, and it looks like a real little movie (but with no sound).

I shoot movies when we go to Death Valley, and to the William S. Hart Ranch (he was a cowboy star in silent movies), and to William Randolph Hearst's Castle (someone made a movie *about* Hearst, but Hearst didn't like the movie). I even held the camera once when I rode on a mule—bump, bump, bump! When you hold our film up to the light, you can see little pictures. But the film Michael's dad brought us has nothing on it; it's just see-through plastic. "Where's the camera?" I ask. He didn't bring one—MGM wouldn't let him.

That was mean. "Can we go there on a field trip?" No, you can only go there if you work there!

Michael's dad says we can make a movie with the film he brought. I raise my hand and ask, "How? We held the film up to the light before it was developed, and that ruins it!" Michael's dad is mad at me, and tells Miss Hall to tell me not to ask any more questions. I hate school! They always do things like that—they get mad if you don't ask questions, and then, when you do, they tell you to be quiet!

Miss Hall says we can draw on the film with colored markers, and then show it on the classroom movie screen. But I can't draw! Miss Hall hands out the film. We each get a piece three feet long. How can we make a movie out of one little piece? It'll last only about three seconds! Our home movies are three minutes long, and Dad sometimes splices together a few rolls and puts them on a reel as big as one of our salad plates; then, we have a 12-minute movie. A one-minute movie is 20 times longer than this piece of film Miss Hall gave me. *Wait. . . there are 20 kids in the class. . .* The bell rings—we'll make our films tomorrow.

I run home and empty my Beethoven bank (I got a plastic Beethoven bust because I learned twenty piano pieces. I cut a hole in the bottom and use Mom's wine cork to stop the coins from falling out. I have money because I babysit). The next morning, I bring my money to class, and before the bell rings, I give each kid a quarter for their film, and they have to promise not to tell Miss Hall; they have to tell her, "Maria Lopez stole it!" (Maria is a fourth grader who steals little kids' lunches all the time. I hope Miss Hall will send Maria to the principal.) I *never* do anything wrong. I am quiet during nap time, even though I'm never tired. And I listen to Miss Hall and I always know the answers and I never break anything. But I *have* to have the film!

Michael's dad left extra film, so all the kids get another piece. I sneak my Dad's splicing tape under the table and tape together the strips. I have lots of ideas, but I decide to make a movie called *The Rocks Go on a Picnic*, because I *can* draw a rock, and a hill and trees.

The Rock family are having a picnic, and then a bully rock rolls in and smashes their nice picnic. So the Rock family calls to their friends at the top of the hill for help, and their rock friends use gravity to roll themselves down the hill and smash the bad rock into dust. Then the Rocks are happy again and eat Rocky Road ice cream

Miss Hall starts the *slide* projector, takes Michael's film, and puts it in the projector like a slide show, showing just one frame at a time! Then Miss Hall says, ". . . and now, we'll show Jürgen [that's me]'s movie." That's right, my *mov*-ie. I've used one of Mom's empty thread spools as the core, and two dinner plates to hold the film together. Miss Hall gasps and says, "What's *that?*" I say, "My movie!" I hope she'll be so happy with my epic, she'll not ask how I got all the film. I tell her, "I'll stand on one side of the projector and hold the film, and Miss Hall, you stand there and pull the film through the projector, *fast*—24 frames per second!" Miss Hall says, "What have you *done?*" I say, "I made a *real* movie." (I try to say "*reel* movie," but that's only funny if you see it written.) Miss Hall says, "You were supposed to make a movie like Michael!" I say, "Michael didn't make a *movie*—he made a *slide* show. So, here, you hold the film here, and I'll-"

Miss Hall takes away my movie, and tells me to sit down. She shows all the other kids' rotten films—*ZZZzzzzzzz*. Their "movies" have stupid lecturing stories, like, *We should not litter!* and *Be nice to animals!* and just repeating things Miss Hall told us. My classroom is a menagerie of teacher's pets. I made up my *own* story, and she's not even showing it!

The Chocolate Fox

I should have introduced myself! My name is Jürgen Vsych (don't forget the ümläüt! It makes my u look like a smiley face). It's pronounced "Yur-gen Vy-zick." Most people at school call me "Rommel." Most people called Rommel, "The Desert Fox" (not *Dessert* Fox), because he was the smartest German Field Marshal in Africa during World War II. He won many battles, but then he started getting illogical orders from Hitler. Rommel was as logical as Spock on *Star Trek*, so he (Rommel, not Spock) got together with his friends and plotted to get rid of Hitler so no more Germans soldiers would get slaughtered. The plot was discovered. Rommel told Hitler, "Put me on trial—I can prove you are a bad man!" Because Hitler knew Rommel was right and the German people loved Rommel, Hitler made Rommel kill himself by swallowing a cyanide pill—if he hadn't, Hitler would have murdered Rommel's wife and son Manfred. I don't look like Rommel, but my teacher said I'm as crafty as he was, I'm as great a leader as he was, I have the same *fingerspitzengefühl* (that's German for "intuition in the fingers"), I work as fast as he did, my enemies admire me, I like to play in the sandbox, and I'm super-obedient, but would turn on my leaders if I knew they were acting bad. I hope I don't end up like Rommel!

Rommel, The African
Explorer . . .

. . . did someone call
me "schnorrer?"

Paradise

Mom gives me two dollar bills and drives me to the Paradise The-atre near the airport to see *Tom Sawyer*. She says she's read the book, so she's going shopping. I give $2 to the woman in the box office (but she doesn't have a typewriter or a desk, so why is it an office?), and she gives me three quarters back. I go to the snack counter. As the man hands me the popcorn, I realize, for the three quarters the popcorn costs, I could almost see another movie! I lie, "I'm sorry, I don't have enough money." He smiles but his eyebrows go down, like Beethoven's

Tom Sawyer is great! I like the cave scene and Injun Joe and the singing and the kids—some of them are my age. Maybe they work at MGM?! I want to work in a movie, too. I like Jodie Foster the best. She's a big kid—ten years old—and Mom says she's been working since she was *three*. I'm twice that old—I have to hurry! I tell Mom I want to be just like Jodie Foster. Mom says Jodie's mother doesn't work, she just drives Jodie to the set and then drives her home; Mom has to teach Monday through Friday until 3pm, and then she goes to lots of "meatings" with other women. She never takes me, but I can see them in my mind, sitting at a long, long table with cows and pigs roasting on spits, and the women chomping down on big drumsticks, holding the meat with their bare hands like King Henry the Eighth. (I have to stay home and eat t.v. dinners cooked in aluminum foil.)

I watch lots of movies on t.v. Mom and Dad rarely watch movies, just loud t.v. shows when I'm trying to sleep. Dad and I watch *Star Trek* and *Wild Wild West* every Sunday night (even though they're not the stars, Mr. Spock and Artemus Gordon are my favorites). Dad is never mad then. Once in awhile, he'll watch horror movies on *Monster Rally* with me. Before every movie starts, they have words like, "American International Pictures presents. . ." or "20th Century-Fox," with trumpets blaring, or MGM's lion roaring. If I can't work at MGM, maybe I can make movies with Dad's camera. I'm not going to ask Dad, though: when I got a pair of roller-skates, Dad stuck his nose up and said, "If God meant for us to roller-skate, we would have been born with wheels on our feet!" I tilted my nose down and replied, "If God had meant for us to walk, he wouldn't have invented roller-skates!" (That's what Gene Wilder, as Willy Wonka, said.) Dad said I wasn't allowed to talk anymore, unless he asked me something. The only reason I'm here is to bring him tooth-picks after dinner, and take out the trash when he says to.

I ask Mom if I can make a movie. She says, "We make movies all the time on vacations." I say no, a *real* movie, with a *story*! She says yes—*if* I buy the film (it costs six dollars!). So I babysit more and more, even though I can't stand kids. Mom is a nursery school teacher, and all the kids' parents need sitters so they can go to the movies. Then I get $25 for my birthday from Grandmother (Mom's mother— she was born three months after the *Titanic* sank, and she dresses just like Katharine Hepburn). I can make *four* movies!

Mom buys the film at Thrifty Drug. To help me make the movie, I ask Alex from my MGM class (no, not Metro-Goldwyn-Mayer!— "*M*entally *G*ifted *M*inors," our school's program for the smart kids [we get to skip classes on Thursdays and put on plays, read myths and do science experiments]). Alex shoots me while I act. I'm in charge; he has to do what I say. But he has some good ideas, too. And some *bad* ones. So we only do the good ideas! My movie is called *Old Ludwig van Granddad*. It stars me as a girl whose father tells her, "Go buy 'Old Granddad!'" The father tears the picture of a man's bust off a booze label and hands it to his daughter. She goes shopping, and sees a bust of Beethoven in a store window. She thinks Beethoven looks like the picture, so she buys the bust and brings it home. The last shot is of the father's face when he sees the Beethoven bust. I wish I had a sound camera—then, the last shot would be of the house, and you would hear, "*Bam! Smack! Pow! Crash!*" *That* would be funny

The first thing we shoot is "Wroughten Films presents. . . " Alex writes it on a sheet of blue cardboard paper (my handwriting is bad). That's the name of *my* movie company (too bad I don't have a sound camera; then I could have a fanfare, too). When I was learning to read, I tried sounding out the name of a sign I saw on Venice Boule-vard, *W-r-ought I-ron*. Mom said it was pronounced "Rot," and it meant the iron was very good, very well-crafted. Later that after-noon, I went to nursery school and painted with Matilda Gomez.

When Matilda painted a really good picture of a boat, I said, "That's wroughten!" Matilda said, "It is *not!*" and stabbed me in the eye with her paintbrush.

My first artistic battle!

I give the film to Mom to take to Thrifty Drug for developing, and she says, "Six more dollars, please!" *What?!* The film comes back ten days later with a note from the lab in Minnesota (that's a state in the middle of America). The man at the lab wrote, "Very nice little movie! But to make it easier for yourself next time, you can shoot all the scenes you have in one location at the same time, and then go to another location and shoot all the shots you need there, and then later cut them together. You can call me and I'll explain it to you. Sincerely, John Nickolas," and he writes his phone number. Wow! I never thought of that!

I make another film, called *Go To Your Tomb, Young Lady*, about how I turn into a mummy at night and stalk the neighborhood, strangling the bad kids in their beds (I had to spend almost $2 for all the bandages.). It's weird shooting the film out of order. I'm not allowed to use Mom's scissors, so I sneak Dad's toenail clippers from the medicine cabinet and cut the film. When I run it through the projector, the film almost leaps out of the sprockets at every single cut. I ask Mom if I can call Mr. Nickolas. "No! He's in *Minnesota!*"

His phone is so far away, you would have to dial four digits just to get connected to his city. But I can write to him. I write, as neatly as I can, *Dear Misster Nickolas, thank-you four telling me how to make a movie, butt my pearants woen't let me youz sizzers and my Dad's townail clippers do naught work vary well*

A week later, Mr. Nickolas mails me a little splicer with a sharp razor. You put the film in it and *chop*! Then you tape it together. For my birthday and Christmas, I ask for splicing tape, Super-8 film, and a book that teaches you how to become a pilot (I want to fly to different places and make films). But I get no film, and no splicing tape (Mom says, "You can use masking tape!" [Oy, *vey. . . I cannot work under these conditions!*]) Instead, I get a Barbie United Airlines toy cabin that's supposed to teach me how to become a stewardess. (*"Coffee, tea. . . or how about a punch in the mouth?!"*) I don't want to serve booze to people—I want to fly the whole airplane!

Oh, *great . . .*

CHAPTER 2

1974, Age 7

Where No Woman Has Gone Before

I'm going to make a stop motion film, just like *Mad Monster Party!* In our MGM class (*Mentally Grueling Monsters*, Alex calls us), the 6th graders made a film about a chess game, with the chess pieces magically moving all by themselves. I want to make a monster movie, with a Tyrannosaurus Rex. I make up the idea: a new student arrives at our school. He's a Tyrannosaurus from Texas, and he wears a cowboy hat, like he did back home at cowboy school. The kids make fun of him because he has a Texas accent (*"Howdy, y'all!"*) and he's the shortest student in the class (he's only six inches tall). He's also the smartest student because he doesn't watch dumb t.v. shows like *Leave*

it to Beaver—he goes straight to his room after dinner and reads. He's a nice Tyrannosaurus, and he tries to blend in and dress like the other kids (he leaves his cowboy hat at home, even though he gets sunburned easily). The kids are *so* mean to him. They steal his tiny lunch (he's a vegetarian, trying to mend his meat-eating ways; he feels bad because he ate so many of his cow friends back home). The kids don't let him take his turn at bat, and they lock him in a desk drawer.

Finally, Tyrannosaurus has had *enough*! He puts his cowboy hat back on and bites the kids in their Achilles tendons, and they die, die, *die*! Then he's the only student in the class, and he gets the teacher's divided attention and he wins the scholarship to Harvard and lives happily ever after—The End!

A few other kids help make the film—they act and move the props around and bring costumes. I make Tyrannosaurus Tex with Play-Doh, but it's not solid enough. Our MGM teacher buys me better clay. It takes a looooooooonng time to make Tex walk across a room, or just open his mouth. All the kids think I want to play the biggest part—the teacher—but I only want to play the *bad* kid, the meanest one. My favorite people in movies are the bad, *bad* ones—Errol Flynn is okay, but I always root for Basil Rathbone, and Vincent Price, Peter Lorre and Boris Karloff. That's what I want to do—be like Jodie Foster, but kill lots of people!

We shoot all the Tyrannosaurus Tex stuff first, and then the kids' reactions to him. I get the film back from Thrifty Drug with another note from Mr. Nickolas: "Nice little film! But next time, shoot stop-motion indoors. Your lighting continuity will improve." Not even Mom knows what "continuity" means. We had to shoot outdoors because I didn't have any of those big movie lights. Alex and I "edit" the film. Every time Tyrannosaurus Tex comes onscreen, the picture looks jumpy: in one frame, it's bright sunlight; in the next frame, cloudy. Also, Alex was in such a hurry, he didn't wait long enough to press *"Click!"* on the shutter after I moved Tex a fraction of an inch, and there are lots of shots of my hand pulling away from Tex. Ooops!

My heroes!

Some shots have Tex looking in one direction, and when we cut to the kids looking back at him, it doesn't look right. When we show the film to the class, the class laughs—oh, no! Alex runs to the restroom. But after the film, everyone applauds *loud* and the kids say, "Wow!" and "I thought Tyrannosaurus Tex was really alive!" and "You're going to be so *famous* someday!" A few kids hunch their shoulders and say, "You were so *bad*. You were evil!" I say, "Yeah, I was supposed to be—I was the bad kid!" But the kids stay far away from me in the milk line, like they can't understand I was just *acting*!

Dad would hate my movie (he hates everything I do) and not let me use his camera again, so I have to remember not to mention it to Mom, either (any time I do *anything*, Mom rats on me to Dad). I tell my best friend, Tea, that when I grow up, I'm going to make films all the time. She laughs and says, "Oh, yeah, *right*!" I decide not to talk to her anymore about making films. It's *my* secret.

Actually, I decided to be a movie-maker before I even made a film. When I was two and a half, I saw the Moon walk. I wished I could go up with the astronauts and film on the moon (we can put a man on the moon. . . but we can't put a woman on the moon!). When I was five, I went to day camp at the YMCA in the summer when Mom was working. The kids were divided into Group A and Group B. One day, Group A was going to watch a movie while Group B went swimming. Then we'd switch. The YMCA rented a 16mm projector with sound, and we watched *The Bride of Frankenstein*. I loved it! Especially the end, when the Bride came to life, and she opened her eyes and didn't blink, and she saw Boris Karloff and *screamed* and Karloff said, "We belong dead!" and pulled the switch and blew up the castle! *Wow!* I wish Boris Karloff and Elsa Lancaster survived and Dr. Frankenstein and his bride were killed instead—they were whiny and boring.

After the movie, Group A was supposed to go to the pool. . . but I just *had* to see the movie again. So I snuck back into the room with the Group B kids. But during the last scene, the counselor saw me and yelled, "Hey, you're supposed to be swimming!" I whispered, "Shut up—here comes the big part, when she opens her eyes!" The counselor grabbed my arm and tried to pull me out of the room, but I kept watching the screen, and when we got to the door, I held onto the door jam until the castle blew up. So I missed the end titles where Boris Karloff's name was finally revealed. . . but I saw the film twice! Boy, was Mom mad. I didn't get any ice cream that night, and no Hershey's chocolate syrup for the rest of the week! Mom was almost as mad as the time I ruined the *Bedknobs and Broomsticks* phonograph record we borrowed from the Culver City Library. At the beginning of the record, there was this musical instrument playing. It was some kind of pipe, and it was the best thing I had ever heard in my life—so I played it over, and over, and over again, and the needle dug in so much, it ruined the record.

For his birthday, Omama (Dad's Mom in West Virginia) gave Dad a Super-8 Bell & Howell camera, so he could film "that little angel!" She meant *me*, but Dad handed me the camera so I could film *him* and Mom. Dad never takes me to the movies—except once, when Mom made him leave the house because she was having a Tupperware party and it was "for ladies only." He took me to see *Pinnochio*. I was more afraid of Dad than of Monstro. Dad is only nice when we go on trips in our jeep, or when we drive up and down Fox Hills (the foxes always run away from our jeep [how unRommelesque of them!]). Dad likes giving rides to hitchhikers—even the hippies in tie-dyed shirts who are against war (*and Dad was in the Marines!*). On our trips, we always take the camera. I didn't like the shots of Mom and Dad just sitting at picnic tables (*Zzzzzzzzzz*), so now I try to do moving shots like on a Ferris Wheel or Merry-go-Round; or, if people are sitting at a table, I walk around them in a circle. When Mom holds our rifle and shoots pine cones, I film her firing, then SWOOOOSH! fast to the pine cone blowing up. I like shooting with the camera better than with the gun (Dad paints one of the pine cone's needles white, throws it in the air, and I can hit it most of the time. Dad gets really mad the times I miss it. It's wasting bullets). BAM! One shot, and you destroy a pine cone or a beer can. *But* SWOOOSH! and you have a picture that lasts forever! I shoot (film) while I go down a steep hill in Death Valley on my new Radio Flyer red wagon. I crash and cut my knees and dent the wagon. . . but the camera is okay. What a great shot! I can't wait to see it. But I didn't notice that the film had run out. Dad is *furious*.

First Grade—only 12 more years to go?! I *hate* school! I ask Mom if I can skip a year or two ahead. No! Charles Schultz did that, and what happened to him? He became the youngest person in the class, and he had to eat lunch alone and he was miserable. I say, "Yeah. . . and then he created *Peanuts*, and now everyone likes him and wants to eat lunch with him and he's rich, rich, *rich*!" Mom doesn't let me skip ahead. *I hate school!*

Even though I love horror movies and the villains, Mr. Spock is my favorite character (Sherlock Holmes is my second favorite). Dad likes the women on *Star Trek* the best. . . the *women*? They're so *dumb*! The only smart women on the show are Miranda the blind telepath, the Romulan Commander, and T'Pau (she was married to Peter Lorre!). Even Spock's Mom lets Sarek do all the talking.

Ever since the 6th graders in the MGM class made their chess film, we play chess after school. I beat the 6th graders all the time, but they don't get mad at me. Dad brings out his old chess set and makes me play with him. He grins every time he wins (when Dad grins, *run*). Then, when I win, he gets mad. He makes me play him again, and if he thinks I'm losing on purpose, he knocks all the pieces over and we have to start again. We play again, and again, and again. Mom says it's way past my bedtime; Dad tells her to shut her mouth, and he makes me play until I'm so tired, I make a mistake. Then he gets mad that I *lost*! I hate Dad even more than I hate school. Dad should go play in Vets Park.

CHAPTER 3

1975, Age 8

Jaws of the Third Kind

Mowed Down

I need more money to make movies. I get 75¢ an hour for babysitting. The boys who live next door get $5 for delivering *The Evening Outlook* on their bikes, and it only takes then an hour to do it—less than an hour when Mom makes me help them (but they never help *me* when I babysit). It's not fair! And babysitting is *way* harder. What do *they* do?—ride their bikes and throw papers into bushes. You have to really take care of the kids when you sit. . . *sit?* You have to chase them all over the house to make sure they don't knock things over, clean up after them, and pay attention to them even when they're boring you to death. The boys can't babysit because they can't pay attention for more than ten seconds; they would just wander off to go play baseball, and the kids would run into the street (or, maybe, the boys are so *smart*, they *pretend* they can't pay attention, so they're off the hook, and the girls have to do all the dirty work!).

Last year, I had a great idea—mowing lawns! We had a push mower. The boys down the street had a gas mower that smelled. I knocked on doors and said, "I can mow your lawn!" but the neighbors said they wanted a boy with a gas-powered mower. I said, "But mine is *quiet*, and it doesn't make pollution!" Mom told me girls can do anything boys can. That's not true. We're better! Tea and I can pitch and catch better than the boys, but we always get stuck playing second and third base. Maybe Mom meant, "Girls *can* do anything boys can, but they won't *get* to!"

So, I bought a gas-powered lawn mower. It took almost a year to save the money (with the money I spent, I could have made 20 movies!). Then, all the neighbors said, "We *told* you, we want a *boy* with a gas-powered mower!" What a bunch of jerks!

At school, we watch 16mm films—mostly documentaries like *Disney's True Life Adventures*. Animals are okay, but I like actors better. Mom takes me to see my first grown-up movie, *The Great Waldo Pepper*. She likes Robert Redford. I like the airplanes. In the middle of the movie, Robert Redford's girlfriend walks out on the wing for a stunt, and she freezes with fright: she's too scared to come back to the cockpit. So Redford has to help her get off the wing. Redford gets close, and holds his hand out, and is going to rescue her—but she puts her hand out, and she falls! I'm not supposed to talk during a movie, but I *have* to whisper to Mom, "What happened to the lady?" Mom whispers, "She fell." I can't pay attention to the rest of the movie. After it ends, I ask Mom again, "What happened to the lady?" "She fell." "No, what *happened?*" Mom says, "She died." I don't want to be an actor! I hope Jodie Foster doesn't die. I want to write to Jodie and tell her to be careful, but Mom says she doesn't know her address. I say, "We could drop off a letter at Walt Disney Pictures" (they made *Napoleon and Samantha*). Mom says that's a long drive.

We fly to West Virginia to see Omama. She loves me to death— "My little angel!" (A teacher once called me a devil. Which of them is right?)

Note the angels' halo (a film reel! I must be the *angel!*)

Omama always gives me presents, even though it's not my birthday or Christmas (my birthday is *way* too close to Christmas). Everyday, we go to parks, to plays, to musical concerts, or the zoo. She even lets me eat chocolate cake—for breakfast! I want to see a new movie called *Jaws*. It's about sharks, my third favorite animal (after killer whales and Tyrannosauri). Mom says "No, it's too scary!"

Omama tells Mom and Dad she's taking me swimming. I put on my swimsuit and we get in the car. . . but we drive towards downtown. When I remind Omama, "The pool's the other way!" she just smiles. We get out of the car, and walk towards a movie theatre. Omama says, "Your Mom would be too scared, but I know *you* won't." *JAWS*! The man who tears our tickets sees my swimsuit and says to Omama, "Your granddaughter dressed for the film!" *Jaws* is so good, the best movie I've ever see—even better than *The Bride of Frankenstein*! Omama says the actors on the screen didn't really get eaten, they just pretended to get bit. They work hard and have to get up early to have makeup put on, but it's fun. They have to learn their lines and not look at the camera or touch their makeup (it would come off). Before we get back to her apartment, we stop at a drinking fountain and Omama puts water all over my hair. When we get home, Mom asks me, "Did you have a good swim?"

That night, because I was good and didn't tell anyone I saw the movie, Omama gives me a clipping from *Newsweek* magazine that has a picture of the man who made the movie, Steven Spielberg, who stands next to a real live dead shark, and wears a baseball cap (they must have had a ball game after work that day). Omama says, "He's a very young man," but he looks like a grown-up to me. I say, "I'm going to be a movie person, too!" Omama says, "That's a *very good* idea!"

When we go to the park the next day, we see a black man playing a trumpet. Omama gives me a quarter, and tells me to put it in the hat on the ground in front of the man. The man stops blowing and says, "Thank you!" and then plays again. Omama's tells me, "If we didn't give him some money, he wouldn't be able to play his trumpet; he would have to be a janitor, or open doors for people at a hotel. It takes a lot of money to make your dreams come true." She tells me *her* dream is to buy a motor home, and travel all around America, "and one day, I'm going to come over to your house, pick you up, and drive you to wonderful, wonderful places—maybe even to Canada!"

The day we fly home, Omama gives me a big plastic shark piggy bank, so I can put my quarters in it to save money to make movies. I put the shark in my room, on top of the piano, next to my Beethoven bank (everyone is surprised our piano is in my room, not the livingroom. Dad hates the "noise").

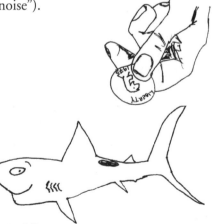

Dad takes me in the jeep to Fox Hills, but we can't ride around there anymore—they're building a big shopping mall with three levels. I risk death and speak to Dad: "Did they take the foxes to the zoo?" Dad says no, they killed them; it was cheaper than rounding them up and feeding them.

Rommel Longstockings

One grade down, eleven to go! I'm in a new experimental classroom—we can do whatever we want in the morning (as long as it's not *too* fun—i.e. no movie-making). I read all the English textbooks for grades 2-6 in two weeks. Then, I get big fat books from Ms. Kitt (not Miss or Mrs. Why do women have to reveal if they're married, and Misters don't?). I like reading about World War II the best. Tea and my Polish friends have big brothers who don't play with their G.I. Joes anymore, so we play G.I. Joe, G.I. Jap and G.I. Spaghetti. We play *Blitzkrieg*, and Rommel puts G.I. Germ and Klaus Barbie in her cardboard Panzer and runs over Poland and Northern Africa. But then G.I. Jew, G.I. Polack and G.I. Pinko fight back, and they send me to a Siberian labor camp, where Stalin brings Rommel the poisoned Tic Tac mint. We have to play when no one is around, or we get yelled at for being "such horrid girls."

A kid I hate tells Maria Lopez that it was *me* who told Miss Hall she stole the film. Maria comes up behind me as I'm walking home and says, "I'm going to kick you're a—!" (She used the "a" word!) I'm scared. So now I walk home the long way so she won't see me. It takes a long time and I miss the cartoon version of *Star Trek*.

On Channel 5's *Family Film Festival*, Tom Hatten hosts *Pippi Longstockings*. Pippi can fight, and even beat up the boys. She lifts dumbbells to get strong. I make dumbbells with soup cans filled with sand and lift them up and down. I put our old foam mattress against our peach tree and kick it, over and over again. On *Family Film Festival*, Mr. Hatten explains how they made the movie. He says in the old days at MGM, when the actors weren't making a film, they had singing, dancing and fencing lessons. We don't have many phonograph records, just Harry Belafonte and Beverly Sills (is she from Beverly Hills?). I try imitating them. I make a sword from an old broom handle, and a bow and arrow from a tree branch and kite string (it doesn't fire very well. I need a knife to whittle, but Dad won't let me have a weapon).

I go back to walking the short way home. When I see Maria, I go up to her and *POW!* her in the stomach. She cries, and I tell *her*, "*You* walk home the long way! I write stories in my head on my way home, and I don't want to see you and be irritated!" The next day at school, I see Maria making fun of Jonathan Levy. I tell Jonathan if he gives me a quarter every week, I'll beat up Maria if she bothers him. He pays me! Then Saul asks if he gives me a quarter every week, will I protect him from Maria? Then the rest of the Jewish kids pay me a quarter every week—without me even asking! Now, Maria *runs* when she sees me. To thank me for protecting Jonathan, his mother brings me a big stack of potato pancakes and a dreidel. I wish I was Jewish: they get to study foreign languages after school, their parents let them talk and tell jokes at the table, and they get to play the violin and go see Itzhak Perlman. And the food is *great*. (I *hate* Presbyterian food—casseroles and Jell-O salads—yuck!)

I can't wait to be a grown-up—then I won't have to waste time doing swim team and other things I hate (I want to be an ice skater, but Mom doesn't like the cold rink). I want to learn to tap dance so I can make a musical. If you're going to be the person who makes the movie, you should know how to do everything, so when you tell the actors and cameramen what to do, they'll listen to you. And I want to fence and do archery so I can go to the Olympics, and then make a sword film, like the ones with Basil Rathbone. Who wants to make a film about *swimming*? Basil Rathbone only did *Bathing Beauty* because his wife Ouida quit her screenwriting career, got bored and spent all his money throwing parties. When I grow up, I can stay home and make movies all day, instead of having to go to Mom and Dad's friends' houses and sit with their dumb kids while the grownups drink beer and laugh like hyenas.

JURGEN's sword was twisted from his hand and sent flashing over the ballustrade...

CHAPTER 4

1976, Age 9

Der Führer Knows Best

Walt Disney is a big phony!

Omama sent me *Grimms' Fairy Tales* for Christmas. The Brothers Grimm wrote *Snow White* before Walt Disney was even born! Disney just copied it! That's easy—a kindergartner could do that. Coming up with the film idea is the *hard* part. Not only that, Disney cut out the nifty part at the end when the evil Queen has to dance in red-hot iron shoes until she drops dead!

"Wilhelm! He cut ze shoe bit!"
"Shoe? You should see vhat he did to *Cinderella*! Call our agent!"

I am so mad, Mom phones Omama (even though it's expensive). Omama says not to be so mad at Mr. Disney: "Not everyone is lucky enough to have as much imagination as you do!" Omama says her encyclopedia says Disney died the day before I was born, and he was

Irish-German, just like me, "and *you* have an added sprinkling of Scots for flavor! It's a sign—*you're* the one who is going to carry on the tradition of entertaining the girls and boys!"

We're moving to San Diego; Dad quit his job at the bank and bought a used car business. We move into an awful apartment over the garage that has mice (not pet ones). Three days later, Dad says, "Come here. . . uh. . . Jürgen" (he can never remember my name). He says that the man who sold him the business cheated him, and we're moving back to Los Angeles. He says, "You can cry." I'm happy—I get to go back and see my friends again. But Dad says to cry, so I try to cry. I make a sad face, but make no tears. How does Jodie Foster do it? (Onions?)

We move back into our house, and every night Mom and Dad scream at each other. In the morning, I tell Mom to stop screaming, and she tells me, like Thumper's Mom in *Bambi* (but with proper grammar), "If you can't say something nice, don't say anything at all!" So I don't talk at home anymore, except to ask for ice cream.

At the Paradise Theater, I see *Mysterious Monsters*, a documentary about Bigfoot, the Abominable Snowman, and the Loch Ness monster. At the beginning of the Loch Ness section, there's music played by the same instrument that played in the beginning of the movie *Bedknobs and Broomsticks*. I ask the teenage boy who sweeps the lobby floors, "What's that sound?" He says, "It's bagpipes." I want to play the bagpipes! I tell Mom, and she gives me the silent treatment. We drive home, and Mom falls asleep early, even before *M*A*S*H* comes on.

I overhear Dad talking on the phone and telling someone he bought a used Karloff. . . a *what*? (Is that a studio? Are we going to make more films?!) Then I see a flyer on the coffee table: *Car Lot*. Oh. Rats! Dad has a weird accent. He says "torlet" instead of "toilet" and "bidness" for "business," and talks like Chuck Yeager, the test pilot. But Dad went to *college*, and Yeager didn't—Yeager wasn't even allowed to try out for the Mercury Astronaut program. . . just because he didn't go to college! (NASA had an *image* they wanted to project.)

This has been a lousy year. All the bicentennial celebrations were so cheesy (I wish we were still a British colony!). The film I was most looking forward to—*Bugsy Malone*—wasn't very good, even though Jodie was in it.

CHAPTER 5

1977, Age 10

The Woody Allen Marching Band

I quit piano lessons even though I like music; I just hate the sound of our piano (half the notes buzz.). So Mom tells me, "You're going to play the cello." When the school orchestra meets, I ask for a cello, and am handed a huge violin, just like Woody Allen played in *Take the Money and Run*. You have to sit down when you play it (I hate sitting). I ask the conductor if I can play the bagpipes instead. "The *bagpipes? Nooooo!"* I say, "Please?" (I hate begging, but I really want to play them.) The school doesn't even own a pair of bagpipes. Mom wants me to be a great cellist, just like Jacqueline du Pré.

The cello is easy to play, but it hurts my fingers. Mom is happy and says for the first time, "I'm so proud of you!" She even drives me "a long way away" to private lessons (Mom thinks Santa Monica is far away [it's *twenty minutes!*]). My cello teacher is 16 years old, and her parents are divorced (she's so lucky, to get *her* awful dad out of the house). My friend Jenny's parents are divorced. The other kids aren't allowed to play with Jenny, even though she's the prettiest girl in the school, she has a pretty great record collection, and she's pretty smart, too (I'm pretty, too. . . pretty ugly!). The teachers gossip and whisper and say only bad people get divorced, and then the kids become bad and get into trouble and take drugs.

The Mentally Grueling Monsters get a field trip to Universal Studios. Our tram goes through a sound stage, and we see all the props and furniture they use to make a stage look like people really live there. Then they show us how the movie lights are so hot, real ice cream would melt before they yelled "*Action!*" so the actors have to eat mashed potatoes and smile and pretend it's ice cream (that's why actors get paid so much money). In black and white films, they used milk for rain scenes, and Hershey's Chocolate Syrup for blood (at least the actors got *something* tasty). We see the set of *Frankenstein*, and we go across a shaking bridge (the same one Jamie ran across in *The Bionic Woman*). The tour guide says it's made of a special kind of wood. . . *Hollywood*. . . ar, ar, ar! Then we stop near a hill, and a whole bunch of rocks come rolling down the hill at us, just like in *The Rocks Go on A Picnic*! (Did Universal Studios see my film?) My favorite parts are the new *Jaws* lagoon and the "Greens" department, where they have all kinds of different trees and plants—when you're in there, it's like being out of ugly Los Angeles.

The Queen is Dying

I go to West Virginia with Mom to see Omama (Dad was going to come, but he got sick and went to the hospital). Omama's hair is gone. She had chemotherapy, and she lost her hair, which used to be even thicker than my hair. Her bald head and round white smiling face makes her look like a baby. She has two great wigs, and lets me play with them. She's too tired to go to the amusement park, but she sits in a lounge chair by the pool and watches me, and it's almost as much fun. I like making faces and walking off the diving board with my arms straight out, like Boris Karloff in *Frankenstein*, "*Arrrrr! Arrrr—!*" and then falling in. Omama laughs hardest when I pretend to be a businessman in a suit, carrying a briefcase, walking down the street with my nose in the air: "I'm an im*port*ant man! I have to be at a *meating*, I *chan't* be bothered with little children—*agh!*" and then I fall face-first into the pool. It *hurts*, but I like to make Omama laugh (Donald O'Connor got really bruised when he performed

"Make 'em Laugh" in *Singin' in the Rain*). I don't want to make Omama sad, so I don't tell her that Dad took the shark piggy bank she gave me and fed it to our neighbors' dog (Beethoven got eaten, too).

Omama is too tired to even sit through a movie, but she gives me money to see *Grease*. I like the songs, but I hate the ending. Sandy is a nice girl, but at the end, she dresses like a slut to make Danny like her. But *Danny* doesn't do anything to make Sandy like *him*. I bet Sandy's grades in college are going to drop. She'll spend all her time fixing her hair and trying to squeeze into those skin-tight pants.

Omama tells me she's going to die. She takes me to the graveyard and shows me where she's going to be buried. I like the graveyard—the tombstones with the people's names and words about their lives, and the flowers and the trees. Omama says she's looking forward to death; "I'm going to have a long, beautiful sleep with no pain." She says she's going to put the money that she was saving for a motor home in a safe place for me.

The Kings Are Dead

All the t.v. stations and newspapers talk about Elvis Presley's death. Mom doesn't let me listen to Rock 'n Roll—only Classical—so I don't know his songs. Another famous person, Groucho Marx, dies. Mom says, "Good—he was a dirty old man!" On t.v., they show *A*

Night at the Opera, which I tell Mom is about opera, so she lets me stay home from swimming to watch it. It's great! I love Harpo, but I like Groucho, too, even though I don't understand some of his lines, which I know are supposed to be funny (because there's a pause after he says them, like he's waiting for people in the movie theatre to laugh so they can hear Chico's next line). Tom Hatten shows Marx Brothers movies every weekend on *The Family Film Festival*. He has a book about them, and says that *Horsefeathers* was shot at Occidental College—that's where Mom and Dad went! "Hey Mom—look! See, the Marx Brothers went to your college!" She *still* doesn't want to watch them. Tom Hatten says he borrowed the Marx Brothers book from the Academy of Motion Picture Arts and Sciences Library on Wilshire Boulevard. *Anyone* can go there and look at movie stills and books and old newspaper clippings! I've never seen the Academy Awards (that's the Nobel Prize for movies), because Dad always wants to watch *Bonanza* or *Gunsmoke*. In the Paradise Theater's lobby, they have movie stills from all the "Best Picture" winners (the only one I've seen is *The Sound of Music*). My favorite still is from *The Bridge on the River Kwai*. I could look at Alec Guinness's photo all day long. I ask Mom if I can go to the Academy library. "No, it's too far away!" I can't wait to learn how to drive. Then, I'm going to go everywhere—to the Academy Library, the Museum of Science and Industry—even the Pasadena Rose Gardens!

Everyone loves *Star Wars*, but I think the dialogue is *dumb*: *"Governor Tarkin, I should have expected to find you holding Vader's leash! I recognized your foul stench when I was brought on board. . ."* But I like the music, and it has the best sound effects I've ever heard, and Obi-Wan Kenobi is the best actor I've ever seen. Guess who it is? Alec Guinness! He's a lot older now, and has a beard—that's why I didn't recognize him. I like *Close Encounters of the Third Kind* a lot better then *Star Wars*. Steven Spielberg is a good movie person. I like all the little details his actors do—like when the boy bangs the doll on the crib (boys really do that!); and in *Jaws*, when Richard Dreyfuss crushed the styrofoam cup to make fun of Quint crushing his beer can—you believe the characters are real.

Finally, there's a good t.v. show—*Don Adams's Screen Test*. Actors who haven't been discovered yet do scenes from old movies, and act with famous actors, like Gene Hackman (they did the scene in *Young Frankenstein* when the blind man spills soup in the Monster's lap. I like Mel Brooks almost as much as Steven Spielberg). Some of the undiscovered actors are really good, but Jodie Foster's even better than them, and they're grown-ups! She's great in *Freaky Friday*. Her mom in the film rides Jodie's skateboard. . . hey, that would make a great shot—hold the camera while riding a skateboard! I shoot a lot on roller skates, but it's bumpy, so it doesn't look very good. I tried shooting on a teeter-totter so the camera could go up and down like the big crane on *Don Adams's Screen Test*, but I could only go up a few feet.

Just *guess* what Mom says when I ask for a skateboard. But there's a hospital only a mile away, and they have wheelchairs. Alex says they won't let us borrow one; we're just *kids*. So we sneak in, tell the nurses we're here to visit our grandfather, and we find a chair in the hallway and RUN! In Alex's driveway, I sit in the wheelchair holding the camera, and shoot Alex's dog running. But when the film comes back, it's not smooth, like Spielberg's camera moves. I figure it out— my elbows need to rest on something. Alex takes the wheelchair back, and borrows a rolling bed, just like in the show *Emergency!* I lie on my stomach, rest on my elbows, and shoot. We can even adjust the bed legs and shoot at different heights. The film looks a little better, but it still shakes. When Spielberg moves the camera, it looks like the camera is floating, and it just makes the characters seem energetic, and you don't even notice the camera—unless you're a movie person like me and Alex. And even then, we have to really pay attention and remember to watch for it. Spielberg's scenes are so good, it's easy to forget to study them.

The Bridge on the River Kwai is on t.v. tonight! It's not a kids' film, but Mom says I can watch it. Alec Guinness is so great. He stands up to the Japanese commander. You like the Japanese commander, too (even though he tries to kill Alec), because he has to kill himself (like Rommel) if he fails to build the bridge. But the movie is 3 hours long, and it starts at 9pm. I have to go to sleep after Alec is released from "the oven." The best movies are on *Movies 'til Dawn* at 1am.

Dad yells every night. Dad's Dad dies (he was divorced from Omama. . . *bad people!*), and we bring home all his electronic equipment; we *finally* get a color t.v. But it doesn't fit inside our credenza, so Dad puts it in the corner of the livingroom, *behind* me. We sit at the coffee table when we eat: Mom and Dad sit on the sofa and I sit on the floor, with my back to the t.v. When I try to eat and turn and watch the picture, I drop food in my lap and Dad yells at me (then what the hell is the napkin for?!). So now I just listen to the t.v. God, those laugh tracks are annoying. Mom lets me take our old black and white t.v. into my room. Now, I go to bed at 7pm (before Dad starts yelling, so I sleep through him), then I wake up at 1am and watch *Movies 'til Dawn* (actually, 3am). I use Grandpa's tape recorder and record lots of movies and memorize the soundtracks (I can do *Casablanca* by heart. I need more money to buy cassette tapes). Then I get up at 6am, drink my *Rocky* breakfast (two raw eggs in a glass) and go to the playground before Dad wakes up.

For Christmas, I get a subscription to *Seventeen Magazine*. In the first issue that arrives, they have an article about a girl in Minnesota. A movie crew came to her town, and she wrote them a letter asking if she could watch them make the movie. She became a "gofer" (*"go fer coffee!"*), and she got to watch them make the movie, and at the end, the producer gave her a 35mm still camera! I want 35mm so I practice with different lenses. With my Box Brownie, all I can work on is my frame composition. They must make movies in Los Angeles all the time. I want to do what that girl did. In the *Los Angeles Times*, it says Gene Wilder is going to direct a film called *Haunted Honeymoon*. I want to work on that movie. I look up 20th Century-Fox's address in the phone book, and Mom lets me use her Underwood typewriter to type a business letter. She shows me how to type the date, and indent, and type my name after signing it. If you make a mistake, you have to "X" it out and it looks sloppy. Mom even gives me a stamp (I told her I was writing a get-well letter to Jacqueline du Pré).

CHAPTER 6

1978, Age 11

Female Acting School

And so farewell to you, Queen Helen!

Omama dies. Dad flies to West Virginia for her funeral, and when he comes back, he is *mad*. I think, "Dad, you have the wrong emotion—you're supposed to be *sad*." But if I had said that out loud, he would have put a bullet in my brain. Last month, at a YMCA picnic, he almost killed a guy who was riding around the park on a motorcycle. Dad picked up a baseball bat and took a swing at his head. The guy ducked and Dad fell on the ground. The guy, wisely, just rode away fast. We don't go on trips with the YMCA anymore.

I run home from school every day to see if there's a letter from Gene Wilder. Why is he taking so long? Maybe he didn't get my first letter. The U.S. Post Office stinks! I send him another letter, and write *Personal* in big red letters on the envelope, so 20th Century-Fox will know it's important.

Our school goes to the art museum to see the big King Tut exhibit. While we wait in line, I sing Steve Martin's *King Tut* for the class, and everyone laughs. I try to get them to sing along, but they're too embarrassed: all the kids have turned into such fraidy cats! I can't even get them to act in my films anymore (Alex moved to Chicago). There are no more MGM classes, thanks to Proposition 13 and greedy voters who don't want kids to have libraries and art classes. In the summer, Grandmother takes me to Seattle to see King Tut again. Seattle has a volcano and a monorail and so many pine trees, it's not even like a city.

6th Grade—only one more year, then out of this stinky school and on to junior high. My new teacher, Miss Falls, *looks* like Julie Andrews, but she turns out to be subtly evil, like the villains who smile as they kill and then smile some more. We're studying the American Revolution this year, learning about those evil Lobsterback Red Coats who taxed the poor Americans' tea to death. Miss Falls announces to the other kids, "Jürgen is *British*!" and smiles at me *so* sweetly. I look at the class, and they're ready to tear my head off. Last year, when we studied World War II, I had to keep chanting that pathetic (but true) excuse, "*I vas born in 1966—I vas not responsible!*" Great. . . now, in addition to the Germans, all the kids hate

33

the British, so I'm now 100% Enemy. Miss Falls's most evil deed is to *say* how much she loves my cello playing, but she makes me do extra math that takes hours and leaves me little time to practice the cello. She says I need to become "well-rounded" (yeah, so I'll be a round peg to fit in society's holes!).

1979–Age 12

Dad buys a liquor store in the San Fernando Valley (in Mom's geography, that's about as far away as Jupiter). Mom sold the stock she inherited and gave Dad the money. Mom works all week at the nursery school, and I work all week at school (plus cello lessons, two orchestras, chamber ensemble, and movie-making), and then on weekends, we have to work in the liquor store for Dad. The store is in a bad neighborhood (Dad probably wants to use us as human shields when he gets robbed). Dad makes me stack heavy cases of beer in the cooler and it hurts my wrists so much, I can't practice the cello for the rest of the day (and my left shoulder has started popping out of its socket—it *hurts*). And what do we get for this? Mom gets nothing, and I get a whole big fat whopping *dollar* (wow, how generous! I could get $1.25 *an hour* babysitting). I steal Ding-Dongs and Hostess cupcakes and swallow them whole in the store's "torlet."

At school, the girls are getting dumber by the day. The dumb boys get made fun of all the time, but the dumb girls don't—*if* they're pretty. It used to be fun to compete with the boys. But now the girls lose on purpose and pretend they can't hit the ball anymore: "Oops!" and they blink a lot and smile and shrug. The girls even start losing at jacks—I mean, *jacks?* The ham-handed fat-fingered clumsy oxen boys, who can't even cut a straight line with scissors, beat the crocheting dexterous females? What the HELL is going on?! If the girls get any dumber, they're going to need help crossing the street! "Oh, I can't remember—is it 'Red means Go'? Help me, David—*you're* so *smart!*"

We're constantly being told we've got to study hard, because junior high is going to be *so* much harder. And yet—*yet!* if it may please the court—it's been years since I've heard the question, "What do you want to be when you grow up?" In fact, anyone who dares to make the tiniest declaration of a goal is shot down by his fellows—I say *his*, because, well, do you think in this climate, a girl is going to be so foolish as to declare an *ambition* (except for Rommel—*but she's crazy! She's going to be an actress!*)? So no, don't worry about what you're going to be when you're 21—just worry about your liberal, *well-rounded* education. . . but screw the arts, and focus on science and math, or the Japanese and Russians will bypass us and blow us up and it'll be all *your* fault, you single-minded arty-farty Nazi Lobsterback you!

The Directing Hydra

Miss Falls announces that our class is going to make a film! Of course, I'm going to direct, right? Oh, yeah? Miss Falls holds an election for the director. . . when I'm in orchestra! My name isn't even put on the ballot, and she picks the two kids with the most votes. . . two? That's like having two heads! The winners are Belle and David. Why is Belle qualified? She's the tallest girl in the school (what a great intellectual accomplishment). And David? Yeah, he's good-looking (like you'll see *that* on the screen), but his *taste*? He thinks *Tentacles* is a good movie! To pick a subject for the film, the class has boring "discussions" (that means the kids shout at each other a lot before Miss Falls decides what she wants to do). I tell them my *Luger-Toting Kindergartner* story, about the kid who was sick to death of graham crackers and finger-painting (it dampened his *fingerspitzengefühl*!): "The Kindergartner Who Had *Enough*" (it'll say that on the poster, in small letters under the title, like "We Are Not Alone," or "A long time ago in a galaxy far, far away. . . "). I have the whole idea mapped out. Miss Falls says no; we have to do a film a-*bout* something im*por*tant, with a *mes*sage, like "Keep Your School Clean!"

We have auditions. I get the part of the villain who lives in trash cans (yep, we end up doing the "Keep Your School Clean" sermon—

Zzzzzzzzzz). The Trash King knocks things over and wreaks havoc (just like Dad—my inspiration). David doesn't want me to play the best part, but the rest of the class overrules him—*ha ha!* Belle tells the kids one thing and David tells them another. It's chaos (*duh,* Miss Falls!). During my big scene, David grins evilly: he doesn't care about making a good film, he just wants to make me look like a bad actress. I do the scene and he says, "Do it again." I do, and he says to do it again "different." I say, "How? Worse?" He's wasting film. He and Belle know nothing about movie-making. It was a popularity contest, and I wasn't even allowed to be in the running. At least they're doing the special effect I told them how to do: the kids are at a table eating lunch, and all of a sudden, tons of trash magically appear on the table, like Samantha wiggled her nose in *Bewitched,* or Jennie blinked her eyes in *I Dream of Jennie.* David tells the kids, "Okay, now stop. . . and put the trash on the table. . . and now, okay, look surprised. . . " But he says this so casually, the kids don't stop dead still while I throw the trash on the table; they keep talking and fooling around. David wants everyone to like him (except me), so he always smiles and says that *everything* everyone does is "Great!" My special effect is going to look *stupid.* So, after the second take, when David says "Looked good to me!" I step forward and yell, "We're doing it *again,* and when I say '*freeze*'—you *freeze!* You don't move one muscle, or you're *out* of the movie, you *got that*?! And when I say '*go!*' you react *big,* you go—'*Agh! Where did the trash come from?!*' And Jonathan, forget about Maria Lopez—if you move again, *I'm* going to punch your lights out! Now—*action!*"

I edit the film (I'm the only one who knows how), and the class watches it. I've edited in both David's shot *and* the shot I directed, back-to-back. David's shot is terrible, even worse than the mistakes Alex and I made on *Tyrannosaurus Tex* (it's not even *funny*). Then, we see MY shot, and it's perfect. In fact, it's the best shot I've ever gotten! I just have to do that from now on—make sure the kids do exactly what I want them to do, even if they get mad at me. Tough! (I wonder if Steven Spielberg ever had to yell at Richard Dreyfuss?)

When we show the movie to the parents (with only my good shot cut in), they all say how smart *David* was to invent the special effect! I say, "That was MY idea!" but Miss Falls tells me to be quiet (some feminist *she* is. She ignores the girls in class).

I decide to make *The Luger-Toting Kindergartner* anyway, all by myself. I play the kindergartner, and set up the camera on a stack of encyclopedias (boy, I wish I had a tripod). Because I can't move the camera while I'm acting, I have to have a lot of short shots, and then piece them together to make a scene. One time, a few years ago, I cut up a whole bunch of shots, threw them up in the air and then just grabbed them off the floor without looking and spliced them together. I got some great ideas from that. For example, I had a shot of my cat Spock looking down from a shelf, and then I cut to a shot of me looking up, and it made Spock look a hundred feet tall! But it took a lot of splicing tape, so it was expensive to experiment. I wish Mom and Dad were lawyers; then we'd have more money and they could sue Miss Falls (Amy Love's parents sued the California Youth Soccer Organization, and now girls can play soccer). We can't afford to go to restaurants anymore, and no new clothes. I get laughed at every day for wearing "floods" (too-short pants).

I wish someone would watch my movies. I watch them in my closet with my stuffed animals. No one at school laughs at my jokes anymore, even though I know they're better than when I was little. Now, I have to become as good as Groucho.

Junior high, here I am! And I make a new friend—Cherry Igor (I name everyone after food; and I'm like Frankenstein, so Cherry is my Igor). And she's a moviegoer, like me! She's quieter than me (who isn't?), but smart. And *we're* not feeble wimps. When we take the Presidential Fitness Award test, after 200 push-ups, the P.E. teacher tells us, "Okay, *okay*, you two have proved your point—you pass!" We go to see Spielberg's *1941*. . . oh, dear. . . but we'll stand behind our hero—he'll make a better one next time! We ride our bikes to the new United Artists Theatre that has *six* movie theatres. If you're sneaky, you can buy a ticket to a G-Rated film, and see an R. We see as many R films as we can. . . no, not to see nude women! (Why aren't there ever nude men, *huh?*). Because they're *better*. They've got better stories and realistic dialogue. Our favorite film is *All That Jazz*. It's about Bob Fosse, the director of *Cabaret*, and it shows how Fosse worked hard and slogged away until every detail was exactly right. I want to be just like Fosse—but without the cigarettes, booze, drugs and philandering!

Junior high has orchestra every day! Doc, the music teacher, with his mustache twirled, looks like, acts like, and is as funny as William Powell. He teaches me to play every instrument in the orchestra, and laughs at most of my jokes. His favorite comedians are Laurel and Hardy, and when we have half-days at school, he brings his own 16mm sound projector and films (the school only has video now—yuck! It just looks like t.v.). I ask Doc, "How did such a couth, sophisticated gent like yourself wind up in this hellhole, teaching a bunch of talentless morons like us?" He says he has two kids, and he didn't want to tour constantly, as soloists must. Doc tells me how, in 1972, one of his students taught herself to play jazz trombone from records. When she went to high school, she wanted to join the school's jazz band, but the teacher said, "No girls can play jazz!" She cried and went to Doc, who told her, "Go sit in one day, and keep playing. Don't say a word, but don't leave, either." (Hey, that's great advice for women in any field!) Despite the initial taunts, she was so good they had to keep her. That's my Doc, a man of action! Some men *talk* about being pro-women, but they need to put their hiring practices where their mouths are.

Doc met Groucho! When he was 14, Doc played in the Meremblum orchestras, just like I do now. Groucho came to a rehearsal with his young daughter, and told all the kids in the orchestra how great they sounded. Afterwards, Doc was walking to the bus stop to go home, and he saw Groucho waiting for his limo. Groucho complimented Doc on his playing and offered him a ride home. But Doc politely refused. I yell at Doc, "*You idiot! Why didn't you accept the ride??!*"

I'm not allowed in the chemistry class: I'm told it's full (of boys), ". . . and besides, you're *artistic*!" like I only possess half a brain. I sign up for Metal Shop, but I'm sent to "Home Economics" (it's a cooking class—they don't teach you how to buy a house or manage your finances). I thought, here in junior high, at last, there would be lots of discussions about what we're going to be when we grow up . . . but no, just get those A's, write this paper, follow these directions. They're programming us to be obedient followers. Well, I know how to follow orders; I've lived at my house for the last 12 years. The school doesn't really care if your brain is there, as long as your body shows up for attendance so they can count it and get their tax allotment. The classrooms used to have 25 kids. Now it's 38. Even a "loud" student like me gets lost in the din. And even a teacher as great as Doc isn't really training anyone to be a professional musician. When I tell Doc my secret (that I'm not going to be a cellist; I'm going to be a film director), Doc says, "Good—it pays better!"

Dad often sleeps at the liquor store (or *claims* to sleep there), so when I come home and see no car in the driveway, I think the coast is clear. *But*—just when you relax, he comes home. To prepare for battle, and keep up my violent reputation at school, I enroll in karate at the YMCA. The class is taught by three misogynistic ex-Marine drill sergeants, and I have to break twice the number of bricks to get half the attention as the boys. You'd think after a class, Dad would seem like a pussycat, but no—the karate masters only attack you physically.

If you get at least four A's, you get a field trip to Disneyland. Finally, *some* reward for being smart. God knows it won't get you dates or the respect of your classmates. I have a hard time having fun anymore. Movies are just a brief break—then, I have to go home. . . to

Vsychland . . . the angriest place on Earth!
Come and enjoy our many attractions. . .

Anxietyland—where you can experience the fear of tomorrow!

Pintopia—drive in a 1-mile loop around your house! Careful— if you're rear-ended, your car explodes!

The Haunted Tract House—where ghosts scream and moan, and things go bump and *crash* and #«%£@&§!" in the night!

Jürgen's Scary Adventure—hurry to and from school—look out for those gangs! By age 14, your hair will be snow white!

The King Lear Carousel—endless not-so-merry-go-rounds with a mad monarch!

Frontierland—explore the wilderness of Mar Vista, Santa Monica, and Marina del Rey!

Pirates of Culver City—experience the excitement of drunken neighbors shooting out your windows, stealing the clothes off your clothesline, setting your bushes on fire, and calling you in middle of night with death threats!

Mr. Vsych's Wild Ride—when Mom tells you to slow down, go right ahead and drive 100 miles per hour down Prospect Avenue! Watch Mom and your daughter scream in terror!

Peter Pan's Flight of Fantasy—act like a little boy and imagine you can start your own used car business, despite having no knowledge of cars or running a business—*you can fly, you can fly, you can fly!*

CHAPTER 7

1980, Age 13

Rommel, The Deserted Fox

DEAR ADOLF OUT OF FILM STOP HUNGRY
STOP NEED MORE KLEENEX STOP YOU
SHOULD SEE MY TAN STOP LOVE ERWIN

Rommel is surrounded on all fronts, with no supplies and too many battles to fight. Thanks to Dad, I can't invite anyone over to the house, not even Tea or Cherry Igor. So no one invites *me* over. I could join clubs, but I've already spent three-fourths of my life around people I can't stand, doing things I can't stand, wasting valuable time that could be spent doing "storyboards" (I read in *Film Comment* that Spielberg draws every shot [Alfred Hitchcock did that, too]—and Spielberg can't draw well, either, but stick figures are good enough—phew!).

I'm going to write my first feature! My films have always been short, because my story ideas were short. I can keep everything in my head, but in Hollywood, you have to write it out (a "screenplay") and show it to people. I need money to buy carbon paper and a new typewriter ribbon—I wore out Mom's.

I'm on a strict seafood diet: See Food, Eat Food (that's only funny if you *say* it)—even if it's in the trash can or lying on the ground. Mom stopped buying eggs, so I can't have my *Rocky* breakfast, and

41

the only "food" in the house is a can of Crisco shortening, a stick of margarine, Dad's vodka bottle and Velveeta "cheese" (*yeach!*), and Mom's jug ("economy size") of Paul Masson's wine—a man sells it on t.v. ("*We will sell no wine before it's time*"). Mom says he was a famous film director (is she trying to tell me something? Like, *That's how you're going to wind up—fat and pitching booze on t.v.!*?). Well, at least Mom is helping the director of *Citizen Kane* have a nice fat retirement. Really fat.

The food situation is serious. I can't make enough money to buy film, *and* carbon paper, *and* food. Luckily, I get a job working the cash register in the teacher's cafeteria. Only the lowliest of the lowly kids work in the student cafeteria: the Mexican kids ("the wetbacks") and the "trailer park trash" (*ooops*—Dad's Dad lived in a trailer park!). If anyone saw me working in the student cafeteria, I would have to sit at the back of the classroom (the teachers see a poor kid and automatically think they're stupid). But the teacher's cafeteria is considered elite. Kids usually aren't allowed to cashier, but everyone knows I'm honest (to a fault!). I *love* giving my math teacher the wrong change: she has no sense of humor, so she doesn't get why I can do calculus, but I can't change a one-dollar bill. Dinner is a problem; the cheapest meal costs as much as a movie! So, when lunch is over, I dig in the trash cans outside the cafeteria, conducting my own Howard Carter excavation, unearthing ancient treasures. My Fellow Kids throw away whole apples, sandwiches, even packaged goodies! If anyone sees me, I say loudly in my best English voice, "I *say*, now, where's that con*fou*nded English paper? I must have thrown it out with Mummy's overcooked filet mignon. . . "

I finally come up with an idea for my feature; a shrink drives his patients crazy, and one of his patients is like Gene Wilder in *The Producers*, a wishy-washy nutcase who follows the shrink around and eventually drives the shrink crazy. I work and work and work on *Dr. Sidney Psycho. . .* and it's *horrible*. The dialogue is funny (once in awhile), but the story is stilted, dumb, stupid, boring. . . I hate it! And it's only 68 minutes. I should be able to write a 90-minute feature—I'm *13*! Maybe the sun is frying my brain. I have to write outside (Dad always has the t.v. volume blaring). The only time I've been cool this summer is the two hours Dad locked me in the liquor store cooler when I accidentally dropped a case of beer. The next day, when it was time to go to the store, I told Mom, "I'm not going!" She said, "Oh, yes, you are!" I said, "No, and I'm never going there *again*!" She went to the store and told Dad. Then Dad came home, with his Browning pistol in his belt. I didn't even wait for Hitler to open his mouth (I bet he had a poisoned Tic Tac in his pocket for Rommel—*We can do this the easy way. . .* he would say, holding out the lethal mint. . . *or my way!*). I ran to my room and jumped out the window; I had put our old foam mattress underneath in case I ever had to do this—thank God! I always keep a $5 bill in my sock, so if I have to make a break for it, I can go to the United Artists and get some food.

I'm sick all the time. My schnoz is running like Rommel's (did I somehow catch his diphtheria? I hope it's just the smog). My ears are always infected and I have to keep cotton balls in them so green pus doesn't run down onto my shirt (*that* helps kill my appetite). Everything hurts—all my joints, fingers, toes, hips, even my jaw. Mom ignores me: we do not get sick in this family. We do not miss work, we do not miss school! I sunbathe for hours and feel drugged by the radiation (but if you don't have a suntan, you're obviously a poor kid).

Tea runs away to Oregon. She got thrown out of school when we went to Disneyland and the employee wearing the Goofy suit caught her smoking marijuana on the Matterhorn (why *there*? On the "It's A Small World" ride, I could understand. . .). My dipsomaniac chain-smoking philandering Dad wouldn't let me fraternize with a girl with such loose morals.

I see *The Great Santini*. . . great, I spent my babysitting money for some escapism, and I have to watch Dad on the screen for two hours. I think Dad somehow saw this film decades ago and fancied himself as Robert Duvall's character. He sure failed. He only got the basketball *"Cry!"* scene right. At home, I play Rommel at the end of World War II, stoically taking orders from a madman, biding my time till he self-destructs. I try to watch Dad like he's being projected on a movie screen. Sometimes he plays Peter Pan and he makes me and Mom clap our hands for some mysterious Tinkerbell in his imagination. I pay just enough attention so when my cue comes up to react, I can reply, "Yes, I did it!" or "I'm sorry!" or whatever line Dad wants. At school, I'm getting really good at delivering zingers, so I have to squeeze every fiber in my body, or else something could come shooting out of my mouth, and that'd be the end of the next Walt Disney.

CHAPTER 8

1981, Age 14

Kristallnacht at the House of Usher

No, the *dog* didn't eat my homework. . .

Take Two—my second attempt at writing a feature. I want to go to London, so I'm writing a film that takes place there. It's called *Murder You Say?* and it's a comedy about three detectives who figure out who killed the wealthy husband in the first reel (the maid did it!), but they decide there's no rush to nab her, and they spend the rest of the film wooing the widow. It's much better than *Dr. Sidney Psycho*.

I'm hungry all the time (I even ate my math homework last week— *yummy*, lots of fiber and vitamin B-12!). I have to remind myself not to try too hard during gym, or I'll burn all my fuel and get dizzy by 5th period (orchestra!): one day, after I broke the school district's records for shot-put and running the mile, I stumbled into orchestra, dropped my cello bow four times and couldn't see the music. Doc joked, "Did you have an extra martini at lunch?"

The *L.A. Times* says Steven Spielberg has a new office at MGM (just down the road)! All the magazine articles say Spielberg broke into films by jumping off the tram at Universal Studios and finding a vacant office, and then dressing up in a suit and tie and waving to the guard every day. He learned film techniques by watching directors, like Alfred Hitchcock.

Dad has a huge selection of ties he never wears since he quit the bank. Last month, Seth Cohen's mother took me to Saks Fifth Avenue and bought me a black blazer, slacks and shoes after her son beat me in a cello competition because the judge marked me down for "improper concert attire" (my sweatpants were the nicest clothes I had). After Mrs. Cohen bought me the suit, she bonked her son on the head and said, "Next time, this girl is going to beat you—maybe now, you'll be motivated to *practice*!" When I whined that all the other cellists got Mitzvahs and I got nil, Mrs. Cohen gave me potato pancakes and a medallion that read *Honorary Jew, 1st Class*. Where did that notion that Jews are stingy come from?? When I told Mrs. Cohen, "Thanks. . . and sorry about the war!" she laughed so hard she ripped her girdle.

But back to Spielberg. . . except for *All That Jazz*, all movies portray directors as being big and gruff and forever yelling through megaphones—but all the magazine articles I read about directors making films today say the directors are quiet and shy. Phew; I won't have to strut up and down and brag, "See how *brilliant* I am!"

I circle MGM like a shark and try to figure out where Spielberg's office is. I think it's in the Northwest corner, across from Winchell's Donuts. Good—I can get a cheap meal before I break in, and not get dizzy and go, "Hi, Mr. Spielberg! My name is. . . " *Splat!* on his floor. There are three gates, and the South one looks the least guarded. I wear my suit, and one of Dad's old ties. I think it's better if I don't wave to the guard, or even look at him. I just waltz in, like *of course, I come here all the time*! I'm at MGM, where Katharine Hepburn and Judy Garland worked! Maybe they even walked on the exact same places I'm walking now! I want to stop and look around, but I have to pretend to be too busy walking to my office. In the alleys, there aren't any fancy sets or backdrops, potted trees, camels, or racks of historical costumes, like there always is in movies about movies.

I find the Northwest office building and go in. There aren't any names on the doors! Then I see a guard, and everyone in the building is wearing a name tag. Rats, I didn't think of that. I hurry out of the building and go east, young woman. I'd better come back tomorrow, with a name tag (I'm good at making props). I've never seen anyone else walk in or out of the studio—just driving.

The next day, as I cross the threshold, the guard calls to me, "Miss?" *Aggh!* I give him the Spielberg Smile and Wave, but he walks up to me. "Where are you taking that delivery?" he asks, pointing to Dad's briefcase. I say, "Oh, I don't know the name, I just know his office is in the Northwest corner," which comes flying out of my mouth at 90 mph in some strange accent (twenty minutes later, I'm still debating whether it's Katharine Hepburn in *Bringing Up Baby*, or Rosalind Russell in *His Girl Friday*). "Well," the guard says politely, "all deliveries should go through the East gate." I say thank you, and walk towards the East gate—and past it and then I run North to Venice Boulevard in case they're chasing me.

Should I *write* to Spielberg? Gene Wilder never wrote back. I bet Spielberg gets so many letters, he has a secretary read them, and she might throw mine in the trash. *Murder, You Say?* needs rewriting; I'd rather not show it to him the way it is now. What the hell am I going to do for the rest of the summer? Dad is home a lot, and he sleeps all day on the sofa with the t.v. blaring so loud, I can't concentrate on reading, let alone writing. And you never know when the bastard is going to rise from the sofa, like Moby Dick (*He rises!*). I have to always wear boots in the house because of all the wine glasses hurled against walls—every night is *Kristallnacht*. Mom has to go to J.C. Penny and buy new dishes because Dad broke all their wedding china. "Get plastic!" I tell Mom, and for the first time ever, she listens to me. She even buys me a new long-sleeved shirt! (It's good for covering up all those cigarette burns—lately, Dad has been mistaking my arm for an ashtray.) While I'm on a roll, I tell Mom, "Let's get in the car and drive to Montana—Dad won't find us!" She starts to cry, "I can't—he'll take the house." I say, "Let him have it!" Mom buys me ice cream, and tells me I have to "Think Happy Thoughts!" What, is she *nuts*? If I think *lies* and mentally move to Neverland, I'm going to let my guard down, and get smashed in the head. Mom buys me a 25-cent copy of Anne Frank's diary at the Friends of the Library sale. It's very good. I start keeping my own diary, writing in my "Cello Lessons" notebooks so Dad won't find it. I pretend I'm Anne Frank and I have to stay dead quiet in my room, because Dad is a Nazi who all of a sudden might appear and tear the house apart.

I want to move to New York. *The New York Times* is so much better than the *L.A. Times,* and they have lots of stage theatres, and you don't need a car. My favorite book, *Harriet the Spy*, my favorite G-rated film, *The World of Henry Orient*, and my favorite R-rated film, *All That Jazz*, are set there, and Woody Allen and the Marx Brothers are from there. Everyone says, "It's dirty and dangerous— you don't want to go *there!*"

I take the bus to the Academy of Motion Picture Arts and Sciences Library (in Mom's geography, Venus). You have to give them your I.D. to go in there. I don't have one, so they tell me to bring my parents! I beg, "Please, it took me all morning to get here! If I give you my camera as ransom, will you let me come in? "*Okay*. . . (deep sighs)." Rules, rules, rules! If I obeyed every rule, I would never get a movie made! I read the screenplay of *The Bridge on the River Kwai*. The dialogue is printed in the center of the page. The Librarian lends me a ruler so I can write down how big to make the margins. I also get the Marx Brothers's file—it's huge! I read old newspaper articles about them. You can't check books out (unless you're famous like Tom Hatten), so I have to read fast. I wish I could come here every day!

Now school is only half bad (3 classes out of 6): I see Doc for orchestra and band, and Mrs. Vincent, the history teacher, thinks I'm funny and actually gets my jokes! She likes my poison-pen book reports and my cello-playing (my left shoulder is now popping out of its socket constantly—it *hurts*. My right shoulder pops out, too, but that only affects my baseball-playing). But, unlike Miss Falls, Mrs. Vincent doesn't waste my time with homework that has nothing to do with my goals. She says after college, I should get a no-brainer job (like working at McDonald's), so I'll have lots of energy for my artistic work. During math class, I write to Spielberg and ask for a job as an assistant director on his next film.

Dad crashes his car on the freeway. The roof is totally caved in, but Dad somehow just got out and walked away without a scratch. Every Friday at school, when people say, "See you Monday!" I reply, "Well, maybe. . . " because I honestly don't know if this will be the weekend Dad pulls the trigger.

CHAPTER 9

1982, Age 15

The History of a Young Producer's Blazing Anxiety

"Actually, it's pronounced Yurgen Vy-zick!"

Support Your Local Spielberg

My late Christmas present is a ticket to *A Day in Hollywood, A Night in the Ukraine*. It's great—tap dancing in Act I, then a Marx Brothers musical in Act II. I want to write a musical! Maybe a musical version of *Murder, You Say?* Maybe I should do plays and musicals instead of films. Plays are cheaper to produce, *and* you can charge admission. People won't pay to see a kid's film (unless, like Spielberg, you grow up in a small city. Nobody in L.A. is impressed if a kid makes a film). Which should I do? Just when I was getting good at films!

For an English class assignment, I direct *Macbeth*. I also play one of the murderers (of course). After the show, one of the parents comes up to me and tells me her best friend is a casting director, and I should meet her. I say sorry, but I'm not really interested in fishing. She double takes (like Oliver Hardy), and she says casting directors cast for *actors*, not fish! She asks me, "Do you have a headshot?" A *what*? No, just my cello portrait (I'm always behind the camera, so there are almost no photos of me). The woman tells me they're having a "cattle call" on Monday, and my mother should take me. I'm going to be in a Western! (Maybe I should bring *Tyrannosaurus Tex*?)

I don't even bother asking Mom. I forge a note to the school saying I have to go to the orthodontist, and I take two buses to Century City. The casting office is near 20th Century-Fox, but it's in one of the big triangular towers, not on the lot (rats! I wanted to eat in the commissary). I sit with a lot of other teenagers. Their parents are with them, and they're all studying sheets of paper (dummies, their lips move!). The woman in charge takes my cello photo and hands me some papers, "Here are the sides." Sides of what, bacon? Oh, screenplay pages! I read them. . . *yuck*. The dialogue is so *phony*; it's just a bunch of smart-alecky lines. I wrote better stuff when I was in kindergarten. I see other kids writing on the paper. I ask for a pen, and I rewrite the dialogue so it's more believable and has some subtlety. The scene is about when a girl and boy first meet. The girl's stage directions describe her as "Chrissy, a beautiful girl with blonde hair and a tight blouse. . . " (good thing I have blonde hair—one out of three ain't bad. And *I* can read without moving my lips!). The boy is described as, "John." Yep, that's it. There's nothing in the scene about cowboys. I don't see how this is a Western. . .

A woman who needs to fire her plastic surgeon comes out, squints at a sheet of paper and says, "Jerkin Veeeessh?"

"Actually, it's pronounced *Throatwobbler Mangrove!*" The woman just stares at me (she's obviously not a Monty Python fan).

The director slouches in his chair and wears a baseball cap and jeans (the woman didn't tell me he's the director, but the Spielberg attire tipped me off). I say, "Boy, that dialogue *stank*, didn't it? But I came up with one good line—it was hard without seeing the whole script, but anything would be better than that!" I look up, and the director has that grown-ups' "Oh My God Who Does She Think She Is?" expression, that look I've instilled in most adults since my first day of nursery school. I catch a glimpse of the boy's script. He's just underlined his lines (like those are the only *important* ones). Ooops. Not only were we not supposed to rewrite the script (Humphrey Bogart rewrote a lot of his lines for *Casablanca*), I bet this Spielberg dress-alike wrote it! *Ooops.* "Sorry," I say, inching towards the door, "I think I'm in the wrong profession!" I run out, but stop long enough when I see *donuts* on the table by the door. I grab one—no, two—and run out, licking both of them before they can yell, "Drop those! Unhand our donuts!"

I guess I won't be a great villain like Peter Lorre or Boris Karloff after all. I won't get to act with Alec Guinness. . . but I can *direct* him! That's even better! I'm not going to force *my* actors to come up with decent lines. I'm going to write such good lines, they can just show up, do their scenes, and then go and take tap lessons or practice different accents.

I play Gabriel Fauré's *Elegy* on the cello for the spring concert. I play okay—only one mistake—and get a lot of applause. . . but DAD comes! *Why* did Mom tell him? Oh *God*! He shuffles up the aisle with his dirty shirt hanging out of his pants (well, at least he *wore* pants), and hands me a bunch of roses—the roses I bought for *Doc*! And he's taken off the protective plastic wrapping, so when I take the roses, I get thorns in my index finger and thumb—*Fuck! Owww!* It's a great metaphor for my family—publicly praising me while simultaneously drawing blood. Back in Doc's classroom, Doc hugs me and says, "You were *great!*" The kids, who have all seen Dad, keep their distance. Doc doesn't say anything about Dad, but he does say, "Anytime you want to come over and talk, you can." My lifeline. But I don't want to wear it thin. I want to tell Doc every-thing (*"Get me the fuck out of that house!"*), but he would do something, and Dad would kill him, literally. I can't put Doc in danger like that. For the last few weeks of school, the teachers smile at me sympa-thetically, now that they know Jürgen's parents aren't the suave jet setting couple they had imagined. Some of the kids want to touch the sleeve of the future Mstislav Rostropovich so they can tell their kids, *I knew her!* The majority of the students are dying to jeer, "You might be head of the class, but we know you're the descendant of trash—oh, and by the way: Your mama's *so* fat, she. . . " but they don't dare because the Class Genius and Class Clown is also, annoy-ingly, the Class Jock who wouldn't think twice about smashing their heads into a row of lockers. I play the *Elegy* again at the 9th grade party. None of the kids will talk to me, even after I pull off the *Elegy* ten times better than at the spring concert. Doc records me, and when I listen to the playback, I know I can join the L.A. Philhar-monic and make enough money to pay for an apartment until I break into show business.

Grandmother takes me and Mom to Europe. We go to Lund, Copenhagen, Nürenberg, and Vienna (where, on every other block, I see a plaque on a building reading, "Beethoven lived here!" "Beethoven lived here!" *"No*, Beethoven lived *here!"* Was he running away from his landlords?). We take a boat up the Rhine, visit Köln, then spend four days in London. You don't need a car in London, even though it's bigger than L.A.—they have tons of buses, and an underground train. Grandmother takes us to see *The Pirates of Penzance*; it's even better than *A Day in Hollywood/A Night in the Ukraine*. Groucho Marx liked the show's writers, Gilbert and Sullivan. Groucho even played Ko-Ko in *The Mikado*, on t.v. When I get home, I start working on a musical version of *Murder, You Say?* It goes okay, until Act II. Then I run out of ideas. And it's only halfway done! The second act could be just songs. . . but, about *what*? I'm already said everything I wanted to say. Bleeech!

Mom and I go to the Hollywood Bowl to hear John Williams conduct his movie scores. I bet Spielberg is going to come, too! The Bowl is so big, and we're really far back. In the box seats (they're expensive), I see a man with a beard and glasses sitting with a little blonde girl—I say, "Mom, *Mom*! It's Steven Spielberg and Drew Barrymore!" She says, "Pooh!" Then, someone shines a bright light on the man, like a news camera. I insist, "That's *him*! Can we go down and meet him?" Mom says, "Only the people who have box seats can go down there." I say, "They'll let us go there just to say 'hi!'" Mom says nothing, as usual. *Damn it!* When I'm 18, I'm going to go anywhere I want! The next day, the *Los Angeles Times* reports that Spielberg and Drew Barrymore really enjoyed the concert.

High School Madness

This is what I've been looking forward to all these years? I read the entire English curriculum for the 10th, 11th and 12th grades when I was in the 3rd grade! If I can't go to The Crossroads School for the Arts and Sciences, I wish I could at least go to Granada Hills High— they have *bagpipes* in their band. Mom says, "That's in the Valley!" (aka Jupiter). And no more trips to Disneyland; kids who get four A's go to Magic Mountain—just what I need after a week of thrill rides at home. Give me the Storybook Land ride and the Jungle Cruise; that's about as much excitement as I can take!

Forget the drama department: "We do not do *student* plays! We perform the *class*ics." (*Cheaper by the Dozen*??) Forget about using the drama students (excuse me—*Thespians*): they're all a bunch of hams. Forget about using the auditorium: the social clubs use it every day. Worst of all, forget about working at the teachers' cafeteria: *we are not worthy*. Kids can't even be cashiers in the *student* cafeteria (we *steal*). The only position available is server. . . no *way*, José. . . I am *not* going to have a thousand students throw food at me every day. Man, high school has driven me to use *way* too many italics! What next—excessive use of exclamation marks?!!! At any rate, back to the garbage bins go I. Thank God the girls are dieting! They discard even more food than they did in junior high. As I scrape tuna off a Senior's English paper, I glance at the horrid prose—*Shazam!* *No student can write.* I'm the only kid who *enjoyed* being "punished" by writing essays. I overhear some Seniors moan about having to write their biographies on college applications (talk about writing your own epitaph!). I say, "Hey, *I'll* write it for you—only one buck!" I write a jock's bio, and then his jock friends asks me to write theirs, too. Thank God I'm a fiction writer! Man, I hope my pen doesn't kill a lot of people. . . what if one of these bozos gets into medical school? (*"Pen-i-cillin?" Oh, I thought it said "Placebo!"*)

I can write fictitious biographies of morons, but I can't write real business letters. I ask Mrs. Vincent to help me write a query letter to literary agents. First, she gives me a lecture: "Everything in moderation!" I argue, "Yo-Yo Ma and Midori did not practice in moderation. John Huston did not spend just a few hours each day directing!" Mrs. Vincent sighs, and says in the first paragraph, I should introduce myself and let them know what I've done; in the second, what I can offer them; in the third, what I want from them. The Librarian at AMPAS (Academy of Motion Picture Arts & Sciences) told me about the Writers' Guild, and I walked over there and they gave me (for $1) a list of agents. I write to all 52 agents who have an asterisk by them (that means they'll look at "unsolicited material"). It takes me weeks, and an entire ribbon, to type up all the letters.

This summer, I watched *The Dick Cavett* show on PBS. Spielberg was on the show, and Cavett was such a great host, I watched all his other shows, even though I didn't know who most of the guests were. I liked Truman Capote, Richard Burton and Helene Hanff. Unfortunately, Cavett is on at 12 noon, during school. We had a half-day this week, so I raced home, and there was an Englishman on the show named Dr. Jonathan Miller. He was talking about a medical mini-series he did, and directing Shakespeare plays for the BBC, and Dudley Moore, and something called *Beyond the Fringe*. He was really funny and super-smart. Groucho's t.v. show *You Bet Your Life* is on at 3pm. I drop my 6th period class so I can get home in time to watch it.

I decide to practice my whip-pans so they won't get rusty. But when I pull the trigger, nothing happens. I take the camera to Thrifty Drug, and the man at the counter says I'll have to take it to a camera store, and it will cost a lot of money to fix. Well, I guess that answers the question *Film or Theatre?* But my plays aren't very good. They have some witty lines, but they die by Act III; they don't have the big *Ta-da!* endings all my films had. I study Tennessee Williams and Shakespeare, but I don't think I could ever write anything like that. I like Gilbert and Sullivan, but my lyrics stink. My dialogue isn't half as good as Oscar Wilde's. . .

I get a job gift wrapping at Hunter's Books in Westwood Village. I could have done this job in kindergarten: all I have to do is use scissors and Scotch tape and say "Thank You." I want to be a book-*seller*, but the manager says I'm too young: "What customer would listen to a kid?" (even though I've read most of the books in the cinema, theatre, music, biography, history, psychology and humor sections.) I can borrow all the books I want, but it's pathetic money compared to playing cello at a wedding (Mom won't drive me any-where; she's mad because I dropped out of my high school's driver's ed class [the teacher was a drunk!]).

Ray Bradbury comes to talk about his books at the Culver City Library (he lives in L.A.!). After his talk, the library staff sells his books and Bradbury autographs them for people. The Librarian tells me, "Come on, I'll introduce you!. . . Ray, this is Jürgen, a young writer." Ray asks me, "Do you write science fiction?" I say "No, sorry, only comedy." Ray says, "Oh, good—we need good comedy writers!" I wasn't going to buy a book (I've read all of his at Hunter's), but he was so nice, I decide to buy a copy of *Dandelion Wine*, and he autographs it. Then I realize he didn't come here just to *talk* to us; he came here to make money. Selling books is how he pays his bills and puts his daughters through college (even though *he* didn't go to col-lege). So cough it up, kid! You produced *Dandelion Wine* on the stage and didn't pay him royalties! (In my own defense, the teacher wouldn't let me charge admission.) You didn't even give Mr. Bradbury a chocolate bar!

I owe this man a chocolate bar

Dad crashes his Buick on the freeway. He just walks away without a scratch, *again*. When Mom talks on the phone, I eavesdrop and hear her say she had to "post bail" because Dad got a "DUI." I tell Doc I'm writing a script and I heard someone use that expression: what did it mean? Doc says, "'Driving Under the Influence of Alcohol,' and the person was put in jail and the wife had to pay money to get him out. What kind of film are you writing?" I tell him, "A black comedy." Great, Dad: all we need now is for me to start working in the school cafeteria and to switch from cello to harmonica, and we'll be A-1 Genuine bona fide Poor White Trash!

Only two more years till I'm 18 and I can get out of the house! Everything will fine, once I leave home. I'll get a toaster oven and make my own dinners.

CHAPTER 10

1983, Age 16

Sherlock Jr.

It's Dr. Jonathan Miller's Fault

I make two lists: *Why I Should Stay in School*, and *Why I should Drop Out*. The only thing I can come up with for the first list is *so I can write dumb high school comedies authentically.*

The *T.V. Guide* says Dr. Jonathan Miller is going to be on *Dick Cavett* for a whole week. On Monday morning, I sit in English class, pretending to pay attention, when I realize, if I went home right now, I could see *Dick Cavett*! I leave my books on the desk, race home and turn on the t.v. just as Cavett's theme music begins (*Glitter and Be Gay*, from Leonard Bernstein's *Candide*). Dr. Miller did a Broadway show with Dudley Moore, Peter Cook and Alan Bennett in the 1960's called *Beyond the Fringe*, which was a big hit (I make a note to get Alan Bennett's plays at Samuel French Theatre Bookshop). Dr. Miller studied at Cambridge to be a doctor, and his father hated him working in the theatre (so what? Dr. Miller should realize that parental disapproval is a *good* sign!). Dr. Miller goes to lots of art galleries and lights his scenes like paintings he admires (another note to myself: go to LACMA) and he learned about human behavior from Erving Goffman books (get those from the library). I learn more from this one show than I've learned all year in school. If I dropped out, I'd have more time to read and study and actually learn things. The next morning, Mom knocks on my door and says, "Time to go to school!" I've usually fled the house by 7:15am, so this is the first time in my life I've ever heard those words. Mom has never told me to brush my teeth or go to bed or do my homework since I was six years old (I learned if I didn't do it myself, it wasn't going to get done). Mom cries and tells me I have to go to school and threatens to tell Dad. I say, "Go ahead—I *dare* you!"

Now. . . how am I going to get smarter? I want a private tutor, but they cost $20 an hour. Well, Ray Bradbury didn't go to college, either: he went to the library. I'll do that, too. I start my own self-inflicted education:

English: In addition to rewriting *Murder, You Say?* I go to a section of the library I don't normally venture, close my eyes, grab a book off the shelf and flip through it, maybe even read the whole thing if it interests me. If I can't understand it, I ask the librarian for the children's section equivalent

Math: cello, piano, music theory and composition lessons, and biographies of mathematicians

History: World War II films, biographies of actors, and *The Dick Cavett Show*

Science: biographies of scientists, Carl Sagan's books, and *Nova* on PBS

Art: LACMA and storyboarding

German: audio travel tapes and repeated viewings of *Das Boot*

Gym: karate, fencing and tap-dancing

Home Economics: Mom's required course—every morning, she leaves a note under my door designating which objects in the house require cleaning.

I used to be able to read a book in a few hours, but reading has been difficult ever since Dad smashed me in the head with the plaster cast on his broken arm (I broke it in a fight—hey, he attacked *me*—I was just preserving all that money Mom spent on orthodontia!). My crime?—I didn't adjust the rabbit ears on the t.v. fast enough for him (but I was also stupid: I went off my guard by thinking about Margaret Dumont and Groucho's exchange in *Animal Crackers*, "'But that's big of me!' 'It's bigamee, too'. . . oh they meant *bigamy*, as in two—" *Bam!!* and Dad clobbered me). Two days later, Mom didn't cook dinner hot enough for Dad's exacting standards, so Dad put his pistol against my temple and pulled the trigger ten times (luckily, I threw out all the bullets. . . but boy, was I worried that one was still lodged in the chamber). I've been rather jolly ever since that little incident. . . I mean, how much worse could things get? It's all uphill from now on!

My babysitting career is over. Some little creep third-grader offered her services for only 75 cents an hour (the salary I was making a *decade* ago!), and the parents don't care about letting a non-karate expert 10-year-old who doesn't even have a CPR certificate watch over their most prized possessions, as long as they can save 50 cents an hour. I need money to get an apartment, and to make movies. I can't get wedding and funeral gigs as a cellist unless I have a car and learn to drive. I went on four auditions for tap-dancing shows, but all the choreographers said my legs were too heavy (they looked great for Richard III, but not *42nd Street*). I can't do anything but make movies and music. What else do I like?. . . *detecting*! I get out the Yellow Pages and call "Ace Detectives." I tell them I can follow people around without them noticing me. The woman snarls, "It's called *surveillance*, and if you don't have a car, don't bother us!"—*slam!* By the time I've been rejected by the G's, I decide it'd be better to go to the agencies in person. I take the bus to Beverly Hills, pick the lock of a detective agency's front door (to show them how qualified I am—luckily, I don't get shot in the process), and introduce myself to a man who is smoking at a desk. He refuses to shake my hand and snaps, "Whatda ya want?!" I say, "I want to learn to be a detective, and I'll work for free!" He says, "Here, file this!" and throws a file folder at me. The phone rings: he barks, "Tell them everyone's at lunch!" I take a message from a crying woman who wants to know if we've found her daughter yet. I reassure her, "We'll find her, ma'am, have no fear!" The smoking man pushes a pile of magazines off a cardboard table, tells me to "Sit down and take messages!" and goes to lunch. I guess I got the job!

The next day, Smoking Dick gives me stacks of papers to file, and drinks coffee and chats on the phone to his bookie. When he goes on his 3-hour lunch break, a tall woman who looks like a prostitute comes in to get her paycheck. I ask her who Smoking Dick is. She says he used to be a cop, but he "had to leave" the force. Wow. . . I bet his Lieutenant ordered him to shake down a suspect who *he* knew was innocent, and he refused, and was stripped of his badge. So he formed his own agency, so he could help people without a crushing bureaucracy dictating his actions. . .

Then, Smoking Dick comes in, belches and farts so loud it startles the agency's canary. *Nah*. . . more likely, he stole 200 pounds of cocaine in a raid or tried to rape the Lieutenant's wife at a Christmas party—let's not romanticize, Vsych!

For the next few weeks, I get to see how a real detective agency works. Most of the clients are looking for relatives. We take $400 from them, and the second they're out the door, Smoking Dick has me file the case away, and forgets about it until the clients call and ask if we've found anything. We say we've been so busy, we haven't had a chance to tell them that we've exhausted all roads—we can *certainly* do an expanded search, but it will cost $500 more. Every so often, Smoking Dick will spend a few minutes looking something up on the computer (one of those new small ones, not the kind that takes up a whole room), but usually, we repeat the first scenario and increase the new search fee to $1,300. What a bunch of crooks. I am about to quit, when Smoking Dick hands me a camera and tells me to take photos of a woman and "her companion" having lunch down the road, "and don't get caught!" The camera is a 35mm Pentax with a 500mm zoom lens—I finally get my hands on a SLR camera! I get some great shots. Smoking Dick sees my photos and says, "Christ Almighty, we hired Ingmar Bergman!" He won't let me keep any of the photos for my portfolio, but says, "Hurry up and get your driving license, Ingmar—you're doing surveillance!"

The next day, I go undercover with Smoking Dick. We follow a woman shopping at the Beverly Center. Smoking Dick thought she was going to meet a man for lunch (or some other activity), but no, she's just shopping. Smoking Dick throws a fit and hisses, "Come on, *broad*, call your boyfriend!" I ask him, "What are we supposed to find out?" "Her boyfriend's name!" I walk over to the woman in the bookstore, and tell her she should read *this* book—it's a lot better than the one she's considering. Three minutes later, we say goodbye, and I tell Smoking Dick, "His name is Harry C- and he's allergic to peanuts and that's his credit card she's using, it's a Visa number 42. . . —her finger was over the last four digits—could your computer figure out the rest? And he goes to Gold's Gym every day from 6-7:30pm, and from the smell of things, he wears Old Spice after-shave, and she has one hell of a yeast infection and is trying to cover it up with *Love's Baby Soft*." Smoking Dick takes ten twenty-dollar bills out of his wallet and hands them to me; "Go enroll in Teen Auto School—*now*, Ingmar! Too bad you're not better-looking; we could give you more work."

I had visions of working in the English countryside, rescuing women whose husbands were slowly poisoning them—but it's more like *Chinatown* than *Sherlock Holmes*. They want me to get proof of cheating wives, so their husbands can beat them to death with a clear conscience. When Smoking Dick discovers I can act and do vocal impressions, he tells me to telephone a woman, pretend I'm her best friend, and get the woman to reveal which hotel she'll be staying at in San Diego. I tell Dick, *ooops, I forgot I have a doctor's appointment*, grab my backpack, and run out before Smoking Dick can demand I give his $200 back. I only want to use my powers for *good*, not evil. I go to the library and find books on how to open my own detective agency so I can choose what cases I want to take. All the books say I need to be a policeman first, and get credentials. Join the LAPD? I'd like to live to be 20, thank you! Isn't there any other way?

Well, at least I now have my driver's license (the Academy Librarians are thrilled they don't have to accept my camera as ransom anymore). Mom never goes anywhere after work, so I can drive her Ford Pinto (aka "The Suicide Car") to the Nuart Theatre, where they have a discount card, and a different double bill of classic movies every night of the week. I see my first Chaplin films, *The Gold Rush* and *City Lights*. Chaplin's really good at going from comedy to tragedy. *City Lights's* ending is just as powerful as *The Bridge on the River Kwai*.

Mrs. Vincent said to get a mindless job. Chimney Sweep? (I like wearing a black top hat. . . but sweeping is terrible for your lungs.) I apply for a job at McDonald's: *No high school diploma? Be gone! You are not worthy to flip our USDA ground beef!*

Can I really be a director? Apart from the lack of parental help (Spielberg's mom helped him make props and special effects), I have what it takes: a fast brain, endurance, great vision and Bionic Woman hearing (despite the pus-filled ears), a loud voice to yell *THE SET'S ON FIRE!* and the ability to ignore stars' temper tantrums (*thanks, Dad!*). But my scripts aren't very original. When I sent *Murder, You Say?* to MGM, the woman wrote (on *my* query letter—don't they have their own stationary?), "Very funny, but the Marx Brothers are no longer with us." A lot of teachers said I was so original and creative, but that's just because they didn't see the films I was ripping off.

Fahrenheit 451

One Wednesday afternoon, I come home from the library. Dad is usually never home at this time, but the chimney is smoking. Dad's always cold, even when it's 95 degrees Fahrenheit (lately, he looks like the *Pirates of the Caribbean* skeleton who chugs booze and never stops), so he always turns on the heater and lights a fire. I open the front door, and the livingroom reeks (as usual) and is full of smoke (as usual), but the smoke is thicker than Dad's typical Marlboro Man exhaust. The fire in the fireplace is dying. We ran out of firewood last week. . . what is he using for fuel? Looks like Dad has been making a little crematoria in the fireplace. I wonder if it's Mom? (Ick.) I decide I'd rather not look too closely, and I go to my room. Dad is asleep on the sofa (as usual). As I walk towards my room, I kick something against the heater—*shit*! Phew, Dad's out of it. I look down and see it's an empty Super-8 canister.

I open my door. It looks like the S.S. raided my room: everything is torn off the walls, ripped, broken, smashed, the upright piano is downright, and my closet—there's nothing in it. My closet, where I keep all my work -

I run to the fireplace. A roll of Super-8 film is spilling out of the smoking heap, and the metal spiral binding of my diaries look like broken bedsprings in a junkyard. One page of storyboards has blown out from the flames. My *Honorary Jew 1st Class* medallion is dissolving. Twenty-five rolls of Super-8 film have melted together into one lump. It must have been quite a spectacle. Maybe Dad even wore a cowboy hat for the full effect, and crouched next to the fireplace like Robert Duvall in *Apocalypse Now!* rhapsodizing, *I love the smell of Super-8 film burning in the morning!*

I get in Mom's Suicide Pinto and drive Northeast, stopping at a newsstand to find movie show times. At the Vagabond Theatre in Downtown, I see my first Buster Keaton film, *The Three Ages*. Keaton is even better than the Marx Brothers! He has a clay dinosaur in the Caveman sequence—not historically accurate, but funny. Yeah, like Tyrannosaurus Tex could have really enrolled in my school. . . well, *Tex* is now, alas, no more. *The Three Ages* has survived 60 years. In my house, *Tex* didn't even last 10.

I wonder if Dad is going to wind up like Robert Duvall in *To Kill A Mockingbird*, a harmless idiot who rescues Scout from Bob Ewell? No. . . Dad is going to become Bob Ewell! When I get home, Dad does his impression of Marlon Brando in *Apocalypse Now!* blabbing and rambling on and on and weeping. He's being so melodramatic, I want to tell him, "Take some acting lessons!" (but I keep silent; the psychopath probably has a pistol in his kleenex).

I take theatre courses at a two-year college for kids who were too dumb to get into university. I take voice, make-up and fencing. My arthritis hurts, and I have to save my hands for cello, so I walk around campus with a foil, so I can fight with a weapon instead of my fists. I look weird, but, to paraphrase my karate masters, *Better to be laughed at by 12,000 than carried by 6.*

On the morning of Wroughten Films' 10th birthday (ironically, also the real Rommel's birthday), I wake up with a jolt at 6:07am, feeling deliriously happy and full of energy, even though I went to bed at 5am after a double-bill at the Nuart and then another double-bill on *Movies 'til Dawn.* I attribute it to three restful weeks (Dad has gone AWOL). I lie in bed, planning my day, until half an hour later, when I hear Mom talking on the phone, sounding like her cheery morning self (she has some sort of weird amnesia—she always forgets what happened the previous night, and acts totally surprised when Dad goes berserk every night). Mom hangs up the phone, knocks on my door and calls, "Your Dad died this morning. . . please vacuum the livingroom!" I stutter, ". . . uh, okay, Mom!" I wait for her to go out the front door, into the Suicide Pinto and down the street.

Ya-hoooooo! I scream and leap into the air. . . and I hit my head on the ceiling (my 8-foot-high ceiling. I'm 5 feet tall). I take part of the plaster, loose from the 1970 earthquake, down with me. Wow, adrenaline is a great fuel! Despite Mom's weird, casual life-changing announcement, I know it's true. That 6:07am wake-up was God saying, "Hey kid, the coast is really clear now!" The other teachers at Mom's school bring us tons of chicken, pasta salads, and fruit pies. I've never seen so much food in the house!

CHAPTER 11

1984, Age 17

My Agent
is Committed
(to a psychiatric ward, not to me)

Now I'm the same age as the magazine (which has grown so super-ficial and infantile, it should be called *Thirteen).* I've tried selling my short stories to them, but I haven't written any articles about makeup, dieting or boyfriends, and they don't want fiction, just "stories that address real teen issues." I *totally* forgot about being "Sweet Sixteen." Last year was sour. Maybe I'll be Sweet 61.

The phone rings. . . the 51st Hollywood agent I wrote to wants to represent me! I drive over the mountains to see her (her office is in *North* Hollywood). "You're a baby!" she squeaks when she lays eyes on her newest "talent." She says, "Sign here." I read the four-paged contract, and ask a few questions. I don't understand her answers, but don't want to look stupid, and before she can change her mind about the baby who can't even understand a simple contract, I sign. I ask her, "Where are you going to send my screenplay?" She doesn't have any ideas. . . do *I*? I beg, "[Mel] Brooksfilms!" "*Won*derful idea!" she says, and promises she'll send it to them tomorrow. She shakes my hand and shows me the door. I go home hungry, having not eaten for 24 hours in anticipation of "doing lunch."

"Confidentially, she *stinks!*"

I write more full-length plays: they stink. My *Murder, You Say?* musical is *still* not finished (it's the one thing Dad didn't torch. . . *why, why, why couldn't he have burned* that?!). I like to think I have a talent for everything, but I have zero for playwrighting. I'm still writing at a "Oh isn't she *clever*" kindergarten level. I try wrighting and pounding my head and blowing countless fuses in my cerebral cortex. Should I cry *Uncle!* and spare myself and the world from more bad theatre? Or am I on the verge of a major Shakespearean breakthrough? Ray Bradbury says, "To Fail is to Give Up." I keep working on my musical. . . and finally give up when my sophisticated cat, the lady of the house who would *never* do anything vulgar like bring a dead mouse inside, climbs onto my desk and shits on my manuscript (I always knew cats were intelligent creatures, but never suspected they also possessed such refined critical facilities!).

I have another big *Shazam*: actors go to drama school, painters go to art school, doctors go to medical school—I should go to writing school! I hunt for playwrighting and screenwriting classes. Film schools cost a FORTUNE. You have to have a bachelor's degree to go to the American Film Institute (what *for*?), and the *cost*. . . I could make a feature with the tuition! Anyway, their brochure is so snobby, and it says nothing about getting to direct a feature, or even a short, just scenes—and some of the instructors have made fewer films than I have! (Spielberg went to Long Beach State, but only to avoid winding up in Veterans Park.)

I find a "Young Writers Workshop," an eight-week course that I can almost afford. Since the class description says they teach journalism, Mom, the Newspaper Queen, agrees to pay one-fourth of the tuition. I can't wait to meet young Jane Austens emerging from their attics, fledgling Tolstoys with ink-stained fingers yanking out their hair, nerdy comic book guys writing *Batman* and *Tarzan* sequels. . . The class turns out to be 100% Rich Kids. And I don't mean my kindergarten class's Michael-The-Boy-Whose-Parents-Have-a-Boat rich. I mean kids who casually drop into their conversation, "I left my essay in one of our three houses—either Bel Aire, Beverly Hills, or Encino." I had hoped to make new friends, but I have nothing in common with these Richie Richs; none of the kids actually want to write. Two kids yawn, "My parents made me come—it was either this, or computer camp!" I eat lunch with a cool 12-year-old poet, but his high-flying parents have sent him here to be de-poetzied and turned into an journalist. Poor kid. . . I wouldn't be surprised if he poisoned himself by the time he's 13. Which is worse: two parents who have forgotten you exist, or two parents sitting on your chest every minute of the day? Maybe I was lucky!

When I tell the teacher I want to move to New York, she says she knows a Literary Agent there. Whoa!

Getting The Boot

My agent phones. Brooksfilms rejected *Murder, You Say?* but she's set up an audition for me. I thought writers and directors "take meetings" and only actors audition, but I guess I'm just not getting the hang of Hollywood lingo. The audition is in an office in Hollywood. . . my first trip to Hollywood!

I sit with a group of middle-aged men in the waiting room. They hand me three pages of horribly-written dialogue. I quickly rewrite the blatantly on-the-nose exposition. Because the other guys are just squinting at the pages and moving their lips while reading, but making no notations, I grin to myself. . . *I have this rewrite gig licked*! I enter the room and am introduced to the baseball-capped director (I thought that was going to be *my* job. . . ?). Vacant looks form on his and a woman's face. The Director says to me, "You weren't in dass boooot!"

I reply, "Huh?"

The director says to the woman, "I wanted to see Jergen Procknow!"

I ask, "You mean, the star of *Das Boot* [pronounced 'boat']? And it's pronounced 'Yurgen Prochnov.'" (Man, how did this dummy get to be the director?) I go into my dance: "Well, I guess my agent was so eager to show off her clientele, she just sent her best Jürgen! BUT,

I've played the Mad Hatter, Captain Hook, The Sheriff of Nottingham, The Pirate King, Richard III. . . sure, I can play this middle-aged spy!"

The casting director directs me out of the office. I call my agent and leave a message, but she doesn't call me back.

I decide to move to New York: I've heard that people who work in the theatre have some intelligence. When I tell Mom I am going to New York to be a playwright, her sarcastic response is, "Good luck!" When I ask my Young Writer's Workshop teacher for the name and address of the New York Literary Agent she knows, I get a lecture on the importance of getting a college degree, and she says she'll tell me his name when I get a degree *(Bitch!)*. Everyone I tell about my plans says, "Don't move to New York—it's dirty, dangerous and expensive!" I wonder what New Yorkers say to people moving to L.A. ("Go! They're stupid and uncultured—like you!"). I want to go to Juilliard Extension, or the Manhattan School of Music, so I can learn to write film scores (I pray I don't wind up writing jingles for tampon commercials). I have no idea how you get a hotel room, or make plane ticket reservations. I bet the travel agents are like literary agents—you do all the work, and they charge 10%. I call TWA directly and pay for the ticket by selling Omama's wedding ring, which is the one thing she left me (I wish she had left me her wigs).

My lucrative trade, celloing, is kaput. At my début recital, my left shoulder pops out of its socket, and I can't get it back in. I barely make it through the first movement, then have to walk off. Well, I ended up like Jacqueline du Pré all right. If the arthritis in my feet and hips gets worse, I'm on my way to a wheelchair like her. Even though we do not get sick in our family, I take my dangling arm to the orthopedist. After what seems like a hundred X-rays, the doctor points to my shoulders and proclaims, "*Chronic posterior dislocation—*the worst I've *ever* seen! Hang on, I've got to get my colleague to look at *this!*" Both shoulders will continue to pop out of their sockets for the rest of my life, and the only thing that *might* help is an operation to permanently pull the ligaments and muscles back. The surgery costs $28,000, has an 80% failure rate, and it would make many simple actions, like applauding, impossible. (What a spoil sport I would look like on Oscar night, when someone else wins, and I'm sitting there with my arms at my sides.) "We could have done something five years ago. . . if your parents had brought you in!"

The Big Apple Bites

After paying $20 ransom to get my luggage back from a "porter" who grabbed my suitcases, I arrive at the minus-four star Martha Washington Hotel for Women. I settle in with all the other spinsters, mentally ill women and drug addicts.

Broadway is full of peep-shows and greasy guys leering at you to *"come here!"* I can't stand the noise, especially at night. They say you get used to it, but after four weeks, I'm twitching more than Woody Allen. It's as hot as hell, and my brain melts once it hits 80°. And it's *expensive*: how people can afford to live here, *and* go on vacation, confounds me. I save every dime to see shows. *Little Shop of Horrors*, in a tiny theatre, costs $40 (for that, I could have seen twelve films). *Hurlyburly* and *The Real Thing* don't even come close to Tennessee Williams or Arthur Miller—they're just a lot of posturing and wisecracks (hey, kinda like *my* plays!).

One Flew Over the Agency

I phone my agent. The receptionist connects me to the agency's manager. Over the hullabaloo of two women fighting in the hallway of my hotel, I think I hear the manager say, ". . . your agent has been working very hard. . . committed. . . "

I reply, "She hasn't sent my script to *anyone*—she doesn't seem very committed!"

"No—she's resting! It's a nice clinic with a high recovery rate. . . "

I put two and two together and come up with *I'm screwed*. I can't figure out from my contract if I'm under contract to the nut, or the nut house. The agency manager can't figure it out, either, and he asks me to fly back to L.A. I don't think I should reveal that I'm not exactly someone who can just fly back to L.A. and write it off as a business expense. I tell him, "I'm busy writing a play in New York, but I could possibly return if you set up some 'meetings.'" (In my mind, I can see a long table of female executives ripping my limbs off and chomping down on them. . . *"Mmmm, tastes just like chicken!"*). The manager says the agency "might" continue representing me, but, unfortunately, my agent set fire to her clients' scripts (shades o' Dad). The agency would need to see my work first, and it'll take "the standard six to eight weeks" for them to get back to me. I plead, "Can you make it two weeks? I *am* your *client*." No dice.

It's time to wake up to *reality*, something I've been trained not to pay attention to at home ("Think Happy Thoughts!"): Joseph Papp gets 2,000 plays a year. The only agent in Hollywood who thinks I have talent is in the looney bin. I'm running out of money. My *Murder, You Say?* musical is a Nosferatu. Everyone I meet laughs, "You're so young!" when I tell them my plans, even though I don't feel young at all. I go to an employment agency. Underage, no local references; no job. I decide to go back to L.A. and straighten the agency thing out in person. At least in L.A., I have local babysitting references. How do you get references in a new city? Damn my writing teacher! The literary agent she knows could have helped me somehow, even with a simple reference. I HATE HER! On the plane home, I write about my New York misadventures (at last, a story appropriate for *Seventeen Magazine*!).

La La Land

I call my agency's manager to arrange to meet him and hand him my script, but he doesn't have time to see me. "Write us." I mail my script, call to make sure they got it, and feel guilty for killing the tree. I decide to let my contract run its course. That way, I can tell people, "I have an agent!" I need *something* to distinguish myself from the teenyboppers in Young Writers Workshops, and to make me seem legitimate, even it's an agent who greets me not with *Love ya, baby*! but, *And you are. . . ?*

Seventeen turns down *New York Misadventures*: "Well-written, but it might discourage girls from following their literary dreams." Well, it at least got a rejection letter. . . and written on *their* letterhead (poor little tree). I continue my Sherlock Jr. self-training, and make more discoveries: dropping my mouth open drops my I.Q. fifty points. A sloppy t-shirt and sweat pants render me invisible. Lipstick makes me visible and also makes people smile at me. Jesus, people are dumb.

I go back to the two-year college and take lighting, set construction, singing, advanced makeup and fencing. The other students are all in their 30's and 40's and have been there for years and years, as a hobby (they call me "brat" because I have goals). The Thespians throw parties every few days. I hate their music, the cigarette smoke, the noise and the crowds. The only good thing is the super-fattening food: one meal can fill you up for thirty hours. It's annoying to talk to drunks, who laugh only at the simplest sexual jokes. The money spent on booze alone could finance an entire play. I try to pretend the parties are a one-night performance, but the dialogue sure ain't Noël Coward. At parties, guys who backstabbed you in class now find you attractive (amazing what a couple of cans of beer can do for one's appearance). I keep forcing myself to go to these shindigs because Dr. Jonathan Miller told Dick Cavett that he got directing jobs at parties (*Wanna do an opera, Doc?*). But no jobs come for me at these parties. . . or for anyone else. In fact, no one seems to recall that there even *was* a party, perhaps explaining the need for so many parties.

I decide to try something Chaplinish: just start shooting, and discover things on the set, and then shoot some more stuff, and reshoot if I have to. I can only afford to do this because Cherry Igor's grandfather gave her a VHS camera. The image is bad, but talk about instant gratification! No nail-biting while waiting for the lab to scratch your negative. And it has sound (but nothing to mix the levels). I hope to turn the scenes into a full-length comedy, but no plot materializes. It is also highly impractical, going back to the same locations, trying to get permission to shoot there *again*, and trying to match lighting. Chaplin had his own studio, a crew, and a lot more money than me.

I spend $135 for a one-day seminar called "The Treatment and the Pitch." What a waste of money. I don't want to do business with any producer who can't even read an entire screenplay. I enroll in my two-year college's "Screenwriting 101" class. The instructor reads my script, and gives me a lecture on how I should immediately give up the idea of a film career, "but your typing is excellent! Who knows, maybe you could make it as a secretary!" and asks me to drop the class so a *guy* on the waiting list can get in. I decide to gamble my money one last time, and enroll in a night school's screenwriting course. I submit one of my short screenplays for evaluation before the class meets. My first impression of the professor is that he looks like a typical Hollywood jerk (right in front of us, he chortles with another teacher about how bad the students' writing samples were). But then, midway through his introduction, he says to me, "I read the beginning of your screenplay. I encourage you to keep writing— and I don't encourage many people." The Professor wrote for Disney ("Uncle Walt, a nice man"), but left because he was given smaller and smaller animals to write for (he was ultimately demoted to chipmunk). So he began teaching screenwriting to support his family (note to self: skip the family).

Professor has lots of rules and proverbs. At last, I'll have some technique. I'll not have to rely on 100% inspiration, but I can employ the 90% perspiration/10% inspiration formula every published writer labors under. Finally, I know some *words* to describe how one writes, instead of some unintellectual girly "I just *feel* it" kind of thing (I taught myself how to write features by studying Beethoven's symphonies' structure and pacing). Yeah, now things are really going to get rolling!

My new big goal is to win the Young Playwrights Contest in New York, so I can return there A Star. As I'm pushing 18, this is the last year I can enter. They have only one rule: *No musicals.* Nor do they allow any music within a play. No *music*? I mean, what's the *point*?! My play, *The Necessity of Being Frank*, is about a piano teacher named Frank who is forced to write jingles to pay his rent. I pray they don't reject it for breaking their one rule. I write to the contest committee and tell them I want to direct my own play. I hope this will sway them more towards me, because then they wouldn't have to hire another person. I'm worried that they'll find out that I'm a girl. . . or, think that I'm *not* one! In this era, competitions, colleges and businesses all need a token female—but just *one*, mind you! Two girls won last year, so we're possibly over our quota for the decade.

Except for the occasional movie with Cherry Igor, I've lost all touch with my school acquaintances. Even though I was at the top of the class (and, therefore, worthy of their company), their parents really don't want them associating with The High School Drop-out. When I phone, the once-chatty girls talk only in yeses and noooooos, like I'm a telemarketer. I say, "Tell your parents I'm at college!"

They sneer, "You're not *really*—you're just taking *fun* courses."

I snap, "*You* try spending all night transforming yourself into The Bride of Frankenstein and see how easy it is!" and slam the phone down.

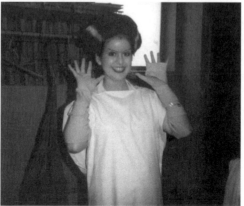

Makeup 201—A+

75

CHAPTER 12

1985, Age 18

The Wrong Stuff

I Sold My Soul for a Velveeta Sandwich

So this is age 18, the magic year I've been waiting for my whole life, when I thought I'd be Free At Last. But I have no money, so no freedom. Mom is now drinking Orson Welles's wine non-stop, but I have to bite my lip, because I need calories and shelter. All my life, I've looked down on prostitutes. . . only to realize *I've* been one my whole life: showing up in class to get straight A's when I should have been at the library doing research, being silent when I should have called the cops on Dad, performing the never-ending vacuuming and cleaning—I've done whatever it takes for room and board.

The war with the Thespian Nazis at the community college has intensified. They don't like this "brat" who has made more short films and produced more plays in the last eight months than they have in eight years. I've wreaked havoc with their pecking order. I hope Hollywood isn't as bad as this college. They're all a bunch of back stabbers—including the *teachers* (I stab people who deserve it, but squarely in the chest: *I'm* not a coward). I ask the teachers, "How do you deal with an actor who is showing up late and destroying the morale of the entire company? How do you handle an idiotic journalist? How do you. . . ?" All I get from them are snickers and "*Don't you know?!*"

Producing *The Necessity of Being Frank* at the college breaks my piggy bank—it's my most expensive production ever: $85. I have to pay $20 just to use the theatre. The bastard in charge of booking the theatre schedules my play for 10am on a Monday. As I turn Lobster Back-red with outrage, he smiles and says, "The students will be nice and refreshed from the weekend!" The day of the final dress rehearsal, the actors don't show: the president of the Theatre Dictatorship has informed them that a rock concert has been scheduled to play at the theatre instead, and my play has been canceled. I sharpen my beak and peck away, throwing my first temper tantrum ever—which works! All it takes is smashing a few photos in the bastard's office with a baseball bat, grabbing him by throat, and giving him a demonstration of my Bride of Frankenstein eardrum-rupturing scream, and the rock concert gets moved to another venue! Sabotage is defeated, and the show goes on. The Thespian Dictatorship sits in the front row with their noses in the air, coughing on key dialogue—until a group of Surfers dump their soft drinks down the Dictators' necks and yell, "Shut up, *man*—this play is, like, *funny*, dudes!"

I decide to retire from acting permanently. I'll miss it, but I figure, for the characters I create, if I can find an actor equal to or better than me, well, when it comes to creating a performance, two heads are better than one. Besides, I would only ever get to play expositional best friends, housekeepers, waitresses and cops. All the comic villains roles are for men (I can't pass for a man anymore.); the villainous women are all tall, thin femme fatales. When there *is* a role for a plain woman, they like to hire a beautiful woman and ugly her up; that way, during the publicity campaign, a pretty face can adorn magazine covers and the press can swoon, "Oooooh, isn't she *brave* to undergo such a transformation!"

The Necessity of Being Frank doesn't get past the semi-finals of the Young Playwrights Contest, although I get an encouraging personal rejection letter from Stephen Sondheim: ". . . a very strong play, with clearly drawn characters, believable dialogue, and something to say." (I bet *Sondheim* liked all the music!) "We would be delighted to receive another manuscript from you [for next year's contest] if you are still under the age of nineteen on July 1, 1986." Nope! I'll no longer be A Young Playwright, so I'll have to compete with Shaw and Shakespeare (I wish I could read some of the stuff they wrote when *they* were 18 and see how I measure up). I enter lots of other contests (they cost $10-$25 to enter). Following Professor's mantras, I try to *plan* my third feature screenplay, not just start writing from "inspiration," which Professor says is a shallow well that will soon dry up. As an original thought has not visited my brain in years, I base my screenplay on *The Necessity of Being Frank*.

I really can't afford to go to the theatre, but I indulge and see *Noises Off*, starring Paxton Whitehead (he replaced Jonathan Miller in *Beyond the Fringe* on Broadway). Whitehead is *brilliant*. Comic perfection!

Writing by the Numbers

My first case of Writer's Block. . . this must mean I'm a *real* writer! I haven't completed anything since I enrolled in Professor's class. For my feature version of *The Necessity of Being Frank*, I jot down lots of snappy lines, but no plot emerges. Professor keeps telling us, "Writing ain't easy," and he keeps boasting that his class has a very high drop-out rate. But *I'm* tough, *I* can take it. Writing was always too easy for me, so now I know I'm really learning things. Professor warns us not to write about things that are too close to us personally. . . *huh?* That goes against the standard wisdom, "Write what you know," and Ray Bradbury's advice to *only* write about things you really love (or hate).

Just when I think I have some signs of life emerging in *Frank*'s outline, Professor orders me to change the main character from the young girl to the older male teacher: "She's not as interesting." It means reworking everything, and changing all characterizations.

I read *Final Dress*, John Houseman's third autobiography (pretty cheeky for a guy who's only 82). Houseman helped create the Julliard School's Drama Division, and he wrote about how he refused to have a class in direction, because "Direction cannot be 'taught.'" I fire off a letter to him: "If direction can't be taught, then how the hell and I supposed to learn it?" Much to my surprise, about two weeks later, I get a letter back (and I didn't even include a SASE!).

April 15, 1985

Dear Mr. Vsych:

Thanks for your letter of March 27th. I maintain my statement that "direction cannot be taught." Direction is something one learns in the course of one's theatrical experience. One does not go into the army as a three-star general; one goes through basic training (acting or technical work in the theater) and when one has mastered one's craft one presumes to tell other people how it is done. My objection is to academically-taught direction.

Sincerely,

[signature]

John Houseman
JH:df

I've been doing that—studying all aspects of theatre. Well, it's nice to know I'm on the right track after all! But I sure ain't at Juilliard: there's not one decent actor in this college. I haven't made any friends here, just lots of enemies, and encounter sexual harassment the likes of which I thought had died out in the 1950's. When I am made the lighting designer for the school's Official Production, the stage manager and construction crew make jokes about my vagina size on the backstage P.A. Men can verbally attack women in ways women can't fight; if you try to answer back likewise, the guys just get turned on and keep attacking. In the past, I've found that smashing a guy in the face and leaving a noticeable mark makes him think twice (*John got his ass kicked by a* GIRL!). But now that we're adults (well, *I* am, at least), this could easily escalate into murder.

One of the stagehands "accidentally" drops a HMI (a big light) on me. I avoid being brained, but the barndoor catches my right ear and almost rips it off. The next day, as my assistant hangs lights, the scaffolding mysteriously collapses. As she lays bleeding on the floor with a fractured skull, three stagehands surround her and gasp, "We thought it was Jürgen up there!"

After I finish programming our computerized lighting system (I *love* Apple Macintosh!), three guys with pantyhose over their heads jump out at me in the hallway. One of them has the stupidity to wear the specially embroidered tights worn by the leading lady of the current musical show, so I quip, "Gee, I wonder which stage-hand has the key to the dressing rooms?" Two of the panty brigade unzip their pants. I have little physical strength after hoisting lights all day, so I quickly grab the arm of the biggest attacker and sink my teeth into his wrist, biting down until I hit the bone (*hmmm. . . tastes just like chicken!*). He screams, and the sight of blood dripping from my mouth is enough to make them all run. I go to campus security to report the attack. With blood still on my chin, the security officer leers, "What did you do to *provoke* them? Were you wearing a low-cut blouse, honey?"

I point to my turtleneck, say, "Yeah, sweetheart," and storm out.

It's not worth the fight. I have *no* chance of doing any decent work in this Little Hollywood. No talent scout in their right mind is going to descend here. . .

Hold on. . . what kind of thinking is this? No, I must stay and fight! If only for the next Jürgen Vsych who comes here and spends all her babysitting money on tuition, only to be driven out by these dogs!. . .

While I'm speaking at a Thespian Nazi rally—er, *meating*—someone in the Guild steals my backpack, which had four library books in it. The school demands I pay $60 to replace the books. I can either not pay the fine and leave the school, or forgo my trip to the Old Globe in San Diego to see John Houseman's production of *Richard III*, starring Paxton Whitehead.

The next Jürgen Vsych will just have to fend for herself.

Paper Chase

Richard III is great! I like Paxton's versatility: from playing Freddie Fellows in *Noises Off* (whose nose bled at the mere mention of violence), to killing off a entire stageful of people as Richard III! I don't get up nerve to talk to Whitehead after the show, but I write him a fan letter.

Back to giftwrapping at Hunter's Books. John Houseman comes to sign *Final Dress*. I thank him for writing to me, and I tell him the situation with my college and ask him, what should I do? He says, "Just start working in a professional theatre. Find a theatre you like and ask for a job." Just like that?! Am I ready for that? I run home and write to Jack O'Brien, the head of the Old Globe. Maybe I could be an usher, and see the shows for free, and learn about different audiences. Maybe after a few months, Paxton might notice me. I could ask him questions about acting. His biography says he's directed a lot of Shaw, too. I don't know how I'd find a place to live, though. A motel?

Chuck Yeager comes to Hunter's to publicize his autobiography. He's a nice man, but he makes my skin crawl; he sounds just like Dad. (Great—*another* nightmare tonight!)

Roll over, Beethoven

I take Professor's screenwriting class for the third time. I have trouble implementing his rules. In class, they sound logical. Then, I go home, whip out the pen. . . and nothing happens. 90% perspiration produces nothing but damp paper.

I see the film version of *Amadeus* eleven times. . . that's *it*! I want to write a film about Beethoven! I've read every biography ever written about Ludwig, so I'm the person to do it! *Shazam! Eureka! Ukiah! That's* something I can write well.

Tonight in class, we're going to pitch concepts, and then hammer stories out of each one. I begin: "It's about Beethoven as a young man, and he. . . "

Professor says, "No."

"Huh?" I think he means I did something wrong in my pitch, like not stand up, or I wore the wrong clothes. . .

"No films about Beethoven. What else you got?"

"What do you mean, 'No films about -'"

"*No! Next!* "

CHAPTER 13

1986, Age 19

Daughter of Python

At last, Hunter's promotes me to Bookseller, and offers me a full-time position. I agree to work three days a week: I'm pounding away eight hours a day at my *The Necessity of Being Frank* feature screenplay and writing letters to every theatre in America—an eight-hour job actually eats away ten hours a day, what with driving to and from work, a mandatory thirty-minute unpaid lunch break, plus the extra time spent bathing and getting dressed (time-wasting activities a writer would usually skip). No wonder the 9-5ers in Professor's class can't save their money to buy time to write, but spend it all on toys to reward themselves for being slaves all day.

After four months of 98% perspiration, I finish *The Necessity of Being Frank.* When I tell Professor, "It's kinda flat, and it seems calculated, like I was following a formula," Professor growls, "That's what re-writing is for!" I feel like I'm beating the script to death. . . or perhaps, beating a Nosferatu so hard it simply appears to be moving. Re-writing just seems to kill my script's original fire. This screenplay took four months to write. Professor says, "That's fast!" (My first two screenplays only took two weeks.)

The Director of the Old Globe Theatre's Young Globe Company calls (!) and asks me to drive down for an interview. On my application, I wrote "UCLA" under "College," and prayed like hell the folks down South would be too broke to call and check (the Globe is constantly having fundraisers). The Young Globe Director says they

have acting apprentices (who are paid half of Equity minimum—
$220 a week!) and unpaid directing interns—but I can't be either,
because I don't have A MASTER'S DEGREE. The Young Globe
Director points out, "And besides, some of our actors are over 65. . .
how do you think they would feel if a 19-year-old gave them direction?" Oh, yeah, I never thought of that. I guess they would be
insulted. "But maybe we can find something for you." He leaves it at
that.

I call and write him once a week for a month. Finally, he says, well,
he needs some help organizing the office. No pay, no title, but maybe
I could see some shows, and even watch a final dress rehearsal! Mom
says, "You're not going!" as I drive away in the Suicide Pinto.

Young Director at Old Globe

When I arrive at the Globe, no one pays much attention to me. I
look around, memorize where everything is, and read about the upcoming season. Paxton Whitehead is going to direct and star in a
revival of Jonathan Miller's (and Peter Cook, Dudley Moore and
Alan Bennett's) *Beyond the Fringe*! I know the play by heart, having
bought the script and both the 1962 and '64 albums. Paxton took
over Miller's role on Broadway and, thanks to the show, he was trans-
formed from a stuck-up *Tennis, anyone?* ingénu to the great comedy
actor he is now. I've just GOT to see a rehearsal!

The Old Globe receptionist finds me a studio apartment for $325
a month, right under the San Diego Airport flight path. I ask to use
the Globe phone to call Mom and ask if any producers or contests
have called me (Phone Call, Good! Mail, Bad. . .). The Y.G. Head
tells me I'm not allowed to use the phone (even though I've seen
everyone else using it to call long distance). Because I might need to
call Professor, or. . . well, I don't know who I would call. . . I go to
Sears and buy one of the fancy push-button models I've begged Mom
to get. I plug it in the wall, but it doesn't work. I return it to the
store, and get another one. . . oh, you have to call the phone com-

pany and ask them to hook it up? The phone company asks, do I have a credit card? What's a credit card? Is it like a gas card?

The next day, the rest of the Young Globers arrive. I thought we would all be teenagers, but these "kids" are old. . . the youngest is 26 (at the Globe, "Young" means "half-priced" or "unpaid"). And they all have MASTER'S degrees. Man, what a waste of time—they could have been treading the boards or, hell, doing commercials and soaps and getting camera experience, instead of aging in classrooms. I impress the actors by knowing where all the bathrooms, dressing rooms and coffee machines are (my first bit of direction!). There's a girl directing intern, Jane, who has *her* Master's from the Young Globe Director's alma mater (what a remarkable coincidence). She's going to be Paxton's Assistant Director for *Beyond the Fringe*. I am impressed and envious, and beg her to tell me all about rehearsals. She seems like an airhead. . . well, maybe she's just tired from the flight over.

Rehearsals begin the next day. While I prepare the Young Glober's scripts, I hear Paxton's baritone voice booming throughout the corridors. I pounce on Jane at 5pm: "How did rehearsals go?" She yawns, "Oh, I only saw a few minutes, I had a doctor's appointment." What?! Man, if *I* were the A.D., I would have to be coughing up blood to miss a rehearsal. How can she be so flippant about missing it?

Way Beyond the Fringe

Every morning, the Y.G. Head has me file scripts and dust the office while he browbeats the acting apprentices. Then he leaves at noon, and I give the acting apprentices pep talks and tell them they're great (and they are), and then I roam the Globe, looking for something to do. Finally, on Day Three, I get up the nerve to sneak into Rehearsal Room B and, knees knocking, introduce myself to Paxton. Paxton remembers my name from my fan letter ("I didn't write back? How rude of me!") and he says of course, I'm very welcome to watch a rehearsal, "if you can stand it!" Paxton loathes rehearsing ("I know you have to do it, but I would rather not"). I'm the opposite: I love rehearsing, then get bored performing it after one week. Paxton has acted in plays that ran for more than a year!

Rehearsals are great! I get to watch the master of comic timing in action. Jane occasionally makes an appearance. I overhear the Stage Manager asking Jane, "Why weren't you in rehearsals yesterday?" Jane says, "Oh, I had to see my friend in San Clemente." *I* come every day, and Paxton, Jim Piddock, Jerry Pavlon and Tom Lacy are more and more friendly to me. We move into the theatre for the last week. Paxton asks me if I can jot down notes he'll whisper to me as he runs up the aisle. Damn, my awful penpersonship! But he can read it (if he squints). On the second day, I jot down some of my own ideas, things I think can be improved onstage when Paxton is running offstage and can't see what's going on behind his back. After the first run-through, Paxton listens to the Stage Manager's notes on potential problems. As he leaves, Paxton smiles and asks me, "Do *you* have any notes for me?" I tear off four pages from my legal pad, and he double-takes. "Thank you!" delivering the line with complete sincerity. Man, what a great actor; he resisted yelling, "How *dare* you!" or "I was being sarcastic, you *fool!*"

The next day, Paxton says hello cheerfully (*phew*, I'm not being thrown out). I hope he'll take at least *one* suggestion of mine. But he doesn't. He takes THREE PAGES' worth! "Got any more?" I give the 49-year-old actor/director another four pages. Over the next few days, from what suggestions he's taking (or not), I start to understand his taste, and he takes about 80% of my ideas from then on—a better batting average than Paxton's beloved New York Mets!

An Old Globe honcho observes the final technical rehearsal and, afterwards, makes some hideous suggestions to Paxton (the Honcho is trying to turn the show into an American sitcom). Paxton knits his brows thoughtfully, squints, looks heavenward, and goes, "Mmmm. *Mmmmm. . .* " But I'm getting to know Paxton, and when I see him suck his cigarette to ash in one inhale, I know *Director Ain't Happy* (and if Director ain't happy, ain't *nobody* happy). I keep waiting for the star of *Camelot, The Pirates of Penzance, Noises Off,* and

Richard III to grind his cigarette into the Honcho's cheek, or yell at him, "God, STOP annoying me with your asinine suggestions!" Paxton simply nods, says "Thank you," and the Honcho leaves. Paxton lights another cigarette. I ask Paxton, quietly, "Are you going to make those changes?" Paxton exhales, "Fuck, no!" rolls his eyes, and goes home to play with his kids.

At the opening night party, I hear Paxton tell the Honcho, "Those suggestions were right on the money." Mel Brooks said in an interview, "Tell the studios, 'Yes, yes'. . . and then do it your way!" Learn from the masters, Vsych.

My Experiences Down the Mine

Paxton's first film, *Back to School*, opens. You know it's a fantasy film when Sally Kirkland dumps Paxton Whitehead for Rodney Dangerfield.

Paxton's two young kids, Sarah and Charles, need a new baby sitter, and I get the job! Luckily, they are way above average children, and rarely bratty. We agreed on $3 an hour, but Paxton either can't do multiplication, or he's just generous and pays me anywhere from $4 to $5 an hour. His wife, Kate, introduces me to their friends as "our baby sitter." Paxton snaps, "She's my assistant—give her credits in their proper order!" Kate is an ace in the kitchen; her chicken, roast beef, and vichyssoise help me grow four inches in two months. Kate is about 6'—just think how my career would improve if Kate had fed me from birth—I could have been as tall as Betty Thomas!

One weekend, when the Padres (baseball team) are playing out of town and the Whiteheads don't require my services, I go back to L.A. to Professor's house for *his* wife's cooking. Professor is in a real snit, barely talking, until a commercial break during *Cheers*, when he suddenly asks me what I would wish for if my fairy Godmother appeared.

"That's easy: to direct one of my feature scripts!"

Professor puffs on his pipe. "That's a nice pipe dream, kiddo, but it ain't gonna happen! It's not going to happen for at least ten years.

You need time just to age." I bite my tongue, and leave. Professor himself admitted he failed at Disney, and was also a failed ballplayer. Screw him! And he only lives in a mansion because his wife inherited a fortune!

Professor calls me the next day and says, "You mad 'cos the Professor stomped on your dreams? Send me your screenplay and I'll make notes on it."

The Two J.V.s

For the second half of the summer season, Paxton plays Benedict in *Much Ado About Nothing*. The Y.G. Head bans me from rehearsals, furious that I usurped his prodigy on *Beyond the Fringe*. I am ordered to *Julius Caesar* rehearsals: "Make yourself useful!" One man was supposed to direct, but he has to replace another actor in a play in L.A., so a woman who has helped with the design takes over. She can't direct actors. Like a mad florist, she arranges, re-arranges and re-re-arranges them in pretty positions. The assistant stage manager's eraser wears out fast. Frustrated, Brutus (John Vickery) asks, "*Why* am I standing here?" She replies: "Oh, you don't want to stand there? Go stand over there!" I was so nervous when I first came to Globe, thinking I would be bringing my little amateurish directing skills to A Real Theatre. . . but my shows were more professional and organized than the Globe's. And the Globe doesn't even give the actors and crew tea and cookies! I am assigned to "run lines" with scowling Vickery (what the hell does *that* mean?. . . oh, he says his lines, I look at the script and make sure he's getting them in the right order). Vickery loves the sun and smoking, and I'm allergic to both. And this adaptation is written in **HELVETICA FONT** in **ALL CAPS**, which my eyes don't like. (I don't know if it's dyslexia, or mere stupidity.) So I go to the bookstore and memorize the Folger version in an afternoon. Unfortunately for Vickery, Folger doesn't have the director's cuts, so I have no idea if Vickery is saying the right lines.

Every night after the show, I follow the cast to a bar. To make up for snapping at me during rehearsals, Vickery buys me soft drinks, and he sticks to Cokes, too: my non-drinking buddy. The actors' tongues loosen up and I get to hear about what they *really* think of the directors. We usually play Trivial Pursuit, and the sugared but sober J.V.s always beat the boozers. If I avoided drinkers, I'd never talk to anyone except Vickery. It's scary watching actors get into their cars after five drinks. The Whiteheads drink like fish, but remain intelligent (they only get weird when fighting about baseball).

G. Wood, the elder statesman of the Globe, who plays Leonato in *Much Ado About Nothing*, stops me backstage during intermission and asks me, "Do you think it would be funnier if I milked the line *Her mother hath many times told me so?*" I tell him no; just totally throw the line away. The next night, he tries it and it gets a better laugh. I bet older actors will take a suggestion from *anyone*, regardless of age, and as long as it's a good suggestion. Why did the Y.G. Head lie to me? (He's probably a failed director.)

Blondes have more fun, but Brunettes get asked for help with crossword puzzles

I decide to take advantage of the Globe's great wig master, Frank Bower, and ask him to improve my naturally blonde hair. People always told me it would turn dark by the time I was in college (wow, college changes you in *every* way!), but it hasn't (maybe they meant a *four-year* college). Frank wants to dye it red, but I don't want to be called "carrots" like *Anne of Green Gables*, so he dyes it black. Several of the male actors whisper to me after I become a brunette, "Oh, Jürgen, it looks so much better—the blonde hair was so phony!" Then they ask me to help with their crossword puzzles, something they've never done before. Amazing how a bottle of black hair dye can appear to raise your I.Q. by fifty points. Lucky for me Paxton's blonde, too, or he would have never listened to me!

I want to stay at the Globe for the Fall season. . . but on new terms. I tell the Y.G. Head I want to be an Official Directing Intern, *and* get paid half of Equity minimum, like the acting apprentices. I think my work is just as valuable, and I'm working triple their hours.

He gives me a vacant look: "You don't have a MASTER'S degree."
Paxton Whitehead thinks I make good suggestions; what the hell else
does this little bastard want?!

So back I go to La-La Land, where, from November to March,
every night is Free Dinner and a Movie. In movie theatre lines, I
hunt for single people bearing Academy of Motion Picture Arts and
Sciences membership cards. I go up to them and whisper, "Please,
may I be your guest?" If the woman says no (and it's always a *woman*
who says no. There's no solidarity in Hollywood, sister), I wait for a
nice old man. Then, when the lights go down, I swipe the woman's
popcorn from those great new popcorn carton holders on the armrests. Life without a student I.D. is harsh, so I always wear the holey
UCLA t-shirt I bought at the Salvation Army, and tell vendors I left
my I.D. in my gym bag. I use Mom's cookie recipe, and take lemons
from Mom's tree, and sell cookies and lemonade in the park. The
cops eye me. I'd better find a new profession. Kids' lemonade stands
are cute, but I look about 34, and that's peddling without a food
license. Digging in Century City Plaza's trash cans always produces a
tasty lunch (lawyers sure know how to eat).

Professor hates my dark hair ("You look like Frankenstein!"). He
gives me notes on only the first eight pages of *Frank*. He *said* he
would read the whole thing. How can he judge my script without
reading *all* of it? Like *Back to the Future*, my script has a longer set-
up, with payoffs in Acts II and III. He says to rewrite the beginning,
and then he'll read more.

Daddy-o!

Terry Gilliam comes to his (and my Mom and Dad's) alma mater,
Occidental College, for the college's 75th anniversary. Terry shows
his work from *Monty Python*, and *Time Bandits*. He talks to the kids
like we're his equals, and talks to the college bigwigs like they're little
kids! Mom, Dad and Gilliam were all Political Science majors: I
raise my hand and ask Terry why a future filmmaker chose that major. He laughs, "Because it had the least number of required courses!"

(Mom always said it was the *hardest* course!) Terry talks with us kids afterwards and autographs lots of coconuts while the school faculty tries to pull him away to "some grown-ups party." I wonder. . . maybe *Terry Gilliam* is really my Dad!? Maybe he and Mom had an affair at their 8-year reunion! (Where else did I get my great comic timing, creativity and love of Vaseline plastic shoes?) I even *look* like Gilliam!

What a resemblance!

I dream big like Gilliam, but I don't even bother writing down my big film ideas: I gotta keep my films small, domestic, and camel-free. I wish I were a painter or novelist; it would be cheaper to break in and actually do some work.

For my birthday, I take myself to see the revival of *Beyond the Fringe* at the L.A. Theatre Center. Paxton, full of rum, forgets he's English and asks me, "How old are you?" I tell him I'm twenty. When Paxton doesn't think I'm listening, I hear him hiss to Tom Lacy, "I've been taking direction from a *teenager*!?!" Tom plops a rum in front of me and says, "You're a big girl now—have a *drink*!"

CHAPTER 14

1987, Age 20

I'm Going to
Kill Gene Hackman

Cinderella Liberated

In keeping with my New Year's Resolution, I inform Mom that I will no longer buy her Orson Welles wine and "enable" her habit. She informs *me*, well then, into the streets you go! (thanks a *bunch*, Al-Alon!). I move into a bachelor apartment surrounded on all six sides by screaming babies. I cook spaghetti in the bathroom sink using the hot water tap, draining the water through an old pair of pantyhose. Then Professor lends me an electric hot plate, and I become a true gourmet, heating up cans of Chef Boyardee and Campbell's chicken noodle soup. The day after I leave home, Mom hires a Mexican woman to clean her house.

At the discount grocery warehouse, I'm envious that a can of Tasty Tuna cat food only costs 25¢, whereas the tuna for humans costs $1.25. I try the Tasty Tuna on Roman Meal bread—a little gag-inducing, but not bad! And because it doesn't taste that great, my stomach says, "Okay, that's enough!" after only a few bites. I cram high-fat foods whenever I get the chance.

I make my weekly pilgrimage to the AMPAS library. I share the elevator with James Woods, the guy who shot Ted Danson, the nice bagpiper in *The Onion Field*. Mistaking me for an Academy voting member, Woods smiles at me and asks about my Del Mar Racetrack t-shirt (such a great actor, he doesn't even turn up his nose when I admit I've never been there, but got it at L'Army d'Salvation). After Woods gets off on the second floor, I go back down to the ground floor and ask the security guard (an independent filmmaker's best friend... or biggest obstacle), "Why is Woods here?" The guard says he's going up to have lunch with an Academy bigwig.

I am not as well-liked by the security guard who rules the Century City Plaza. After fishing me out of the dumpster (I fell in reaching for a 1/8th-eaten Big Mac), he tells me never to come around there again. I need rent, lunch and movie money, and money for hair dye (one sees blonde hair with dark roots all the time in L.A., but black hair with blonde roots looks truly bizarre). I see a "Help Wanted" sign at the Laemmle Monica Four-Plex. Minimum wage pays more than babysitting does, and they have four screens showing foreign films, and all the popcorn and Coke I can eat!

Paxton gets the starring role in a sitcom called *Marblehead Manor*. He's glad to have a regular paycheck; "Nice to get a boost up on the mortgage!" I ask, "Who are you playing?" Paxton snaps, "The *butler*, what else?!" Well, butlers are usually smarter than their employers, so at least he might get a few good zingers.

Oscar nominations are announced: James Woods gets a nod for *Salvador*. I'm starting to see a pattern here...

When researching in the Writer's Guild library, I pick up a Member's Guide. WGA half-hour television minimum salaries are more than I get paid for a year of scooping popcorn. I rarely watch t.v., but sketches are easy to write, so I find the most Monty Pythonesque show, type up some sketches and mail them in. A week later, I get a phone call (Good!) from one of the show's producers, asking me to come in! I take a whole week off Laemmle to write ten more sketches. When I arrive at the office, the producer's eyes bulge. "You're a WOMAN! Oh, how *innnnnn*teresting!"

"Huh? You talked on the phone with me."

"Oh, I thought you were a 14-year-old boy! Weeeellll," the producer says, showing me to the door, "thank you for coming in! Your submission was really nicely typed and professional-looking!" (Now I see why Kathleen Kennedy played incompetent to get out of Spielberg's typing pool.) If only I'd worn a wire, I could have had the evidence for a lawsuit that would have funded my next three films!

Paxton gets me a ticket to *Marblehead Manor*'s Friday night taping at Paramount. The show is moronic and predictable. . . *but*, according to the WGA, I could make $7,000 writing just one episode. My justification for selling out is: I can probably write it in less than a month, and it will support me for the whole year while I write something good. And let's face it, Paxton really needs some decent lines. It only takes a week to write my *Father of the Butler* episode. Paxton likes my script and dialogue, and he gets to give *me* a few notes.

Jürgen Vsych's Gotta Have It

I'm outgrowing my clothes (I thought if I consumed more calories, I'd grow UP), and I can't afford a new wardrobe. I try to join the YMCA, but in their eyes I am no longer a "Young Christian," so I can only afford to come once a week on a pay-per-swim basis. Not wonder the poor are fat.

At Laemmle, a Real-Live director named Spike Lee comes to promote his film, *She's Gotta Have It*. Although I'm disappointed "It" is not artistic excellence, a corner office or a Nobel, the film is funny and energetic. Spike gives the kids working the candy counter t-shirts with his film's logo, which we wear every day (we're all sick of spilling Coke and "butter" on our own clothes), and we tell theatre patrons, "We met the director—he's cool!" Sometimes, the patrons change their minds and go into the theatre showing Spike's film, instead of *Blue Velvet* (God, that film attracts a sick crowd). I tell Spike I've made short films, and I've wanted to make a feature for years. Spike tells me, "Girl, you gotta make your OWN film! NO ONE'S gonna LET YOU—you gotta do it YOURSELF." I think he might be right. His book *Spike Lee's Gotta Have It*, and John Sayles's *Thinking in Pictures: The Making of the Movie Matewan* are my bibles (and they were a lot cheaper than film school!)

Gene Hackman comes to the Laemmle all the time (I presume after a day's shooting—this guy is *never* out of work), and always orders a large popcorn "with extra butter," even though I've warned the great actor that our "butter" is some carcinogenic concoction "approved" by the FDA boys. I scold him, "You're going to have a heart attack, Mr. Hackman!" He laughs, and asks me which films I recommend.

I use the last of my savings to buy a camcorder—my first camera in four years. Unfortunately, I have no ideas for a film. Great, now I have Filmmakers Block, too. I shoot random shots of my stuffed animals, and use my VCR as an editing system, practicing cutting to different kinds of music.

Paxton packs up his clan (or flock; they are not Scots [well, nobody's perfect!]) and they move to Whitehead Manor in Irvine—a house with lemon wallpaper in a new suburban community. Paxton shrugs, "It's the best I can do! If *Marblehead* goes four seasons, *then* we'll start to make lots of rhino!" Spending the day with Paxton's family is the most fun I've had in years (almost as fun as visiting Omama). Miracle of miracles, Paxton and Kate have quit smoking! Kate went through a Stop-Smoking hospital program, then Paxton followed suit (mostly because he was too lazy to go out and buy his own cigarettes). The booze continues to flow freely, but heads remain relatively level. To thank Kate for her cooking, I bring her reading glasses that people lose at Laemmle and save her $6 on store-bought glasses. Paxton muses, "Wilfred Hyde-White is in nursing home. . . now, all I have to do is bide my time until Douglas Seale retires—then, I can get *all* the butler roles!" Yep, things are looking up at Whitehead Manor.

Ah will nehva be hungry a-gain!

I have an old fencing injury that requires surgery (The Nutcracker stabbed me [The Mouse King] in the foot, and a bit of his sword's safety tip broke off and got embedded in my foot, and has been festering for the last two years). It costs a lot to cut it out, but I'm tired of limping, and I don't want to end up like Frida Kahlo. I don't have enough cash for next month's rent, so I give notice, and move into the Pinto. Thank God for McDonald's restrooms, or I would smell like the homeless person I now am. I always wear my cello recital blazer, wash my hair in the sink and dry it under the hand dryers, smiling broadly at the women who come in. In department store cosmetics sections, I put on lipstick and perfume to appear more civilized than I actually am. I now sleep during the last show at Laemmle, and the manager jabs my feet when it's time to leave. My neck is bent out of shape from sleeping in the Suicide Pinto, and I spend half the night worrying that I'll be rear-ended.

Professor lets me housesit when he goes off to the Bahamas (on a teacher's salary? Hmmmm. . .). If Professor throws a fit when I make a grammatical error (err?), God knows what he'd do if I raided his cupboards. So I eat their dog's food, which is *much* better than cat food. One day, it actually rains ("STORM hits L.A.! *News at 11!*"), so I open Professor's entrance hall closet to get an umbrella. On the closet floor, I see a pair of bagpipes. Professor has claimed to be a descendant of Scottish kings. . . but he never mentioned BAG-PIPES! They smell awful, like the sheep rotted decades ago. I blow into the pipes. The bag expands, like a lung. There's a little HUUUMMMMMMmmmmm. How do you get the pipes to stand up straight, like Ted Danson did in *The Onion Field*? I lay them down on the coffee table, blow again, and nearly hyperventilate. Where's the "EEEEE?" I blow HARD. "rrrRRHHHHEEEE!" screech the pipes. I immediately stop blowing, the screeching stops, and the drones slowly expire, "AAAAAaahhhhheeeggg. . . " Jesus, that was LOUD! The next door neighbor comes trudging up the long path to see what just died. I throw the pipes back in the closet, slam the door and run upstairs.

Professor has a friend who's going to New York to write for a soap opera, and he needs a house sitter. Free rent! Or so I think—turns out I have to pay $350 a month. Well, it's better than the Suicide Pinto, and he has four shelves of British videos. And maybe

Marblehead Manor will put me on staff. Things might be looking up at Wroughten Films.

The day I move in, I get my *Marblehead Manor* script back, with a handwritten note from the executive producer saying it "lacks farcical elements that are so essential to the show" (not enough pratfalls and slamming doors, he means). I don't get it—why not just put in more pratfalls?

At Laemmle, our coke-headed obese manager gets men to date her by hiring them as assistant managers, and promoting them over me. When I slip and fall in a puddle of Coke (-a-cola) and ruin my one decent pair of pants (too bad Spike didn't give us an entire wardrobe), it's the last straw. I call Hunter's Books and ask if I can have my old job back. Goodbye free movies, but I get to read, it's a full-time position, and it's a 45-cent-per-hour raise from Laemmle.

The friendly banter Professor and I once had now starts to draw blood. He slams one of my grammatically incorrect stage directions (God, what does that matter? It's not going to be read aloud in the film, and only read by studio heads [who can't read, anyway]). Professor growls, "I get real ticked off when you don't honor the language."

I reply, "You mean, you get *really* ticked off!" (Ha ha! Take *that*, Professor Ph.D.!) Professor doesn't call on me again that night, or walk me to my Suicide Pinto after class; "It's safe!" I guess he figures I can kill would-be rapists with my rapier wit. His friend (the one I'm "house-sitting" for) phones me from New York to inform me that Professor doesn't want to be my mentor anymore. I'm initially devastated (it's just like home—one little jocular "Hey, looks like The Emperor Has No Clothes!" remark, and you're dead meat). . . but then it dawns on me that I've written more than Professor has—three features to his two, and 25 shorts to his five half-hour t.v. shows (all of which he shared credit with other writers). Professor hasn't written anything in years—he lives off his Writer's Guild Award nomination; it got him teaching positions and something to use when introducing himself at parties and WGA panels. And to top it all off, after two years of classes with him, my writing is worse than ever. Perhaps it's good riddance. . .

Another day, another dumpster

I have my first blind date, with a production designer (we can be like Terry Gilliam and Dante Ferreti! I get to be Terry. . .). I saw his ad in the personals. How bad could he be: the guy writes *funny*. But he turns out to be not funny at all in person. He expresses interest in my accomplishments, but after I wax lyrical about my plans for cinematic glory and raise a meatball to my mouth, he raises an eyebrow and says, "You *are* going to give it up when you get married and have kids, right?" My meatball rolls off my fork and onto the table, and I excuse myself. One of the few advantages of being a woman is that when you take your backpack to the restroom, the guy thinks you're just taking your Unmentionable Feminine Supplies with you, and doesn't suspect that you're, in fact, about to crawl out the bathroom window. My fat butt gets stuck, but an understanding anorexic who has just vomited up her lasagna helps push me out. I land in the restaurant's dumpster, which has a 1/4-eaten Chocolate Mousse just *waiting* for me!

Walking to my car after work, a guy in a car stops, rolls down his window, and asks me for directions (goody, I get to practice my craft!). I start to point to the next street, when he suddenly points some sort of Uzi-looking gun at me. I turn and run. I hear a bullet whiz by my head (veterans must have nightmares of that sound). When I get home, I see blood on my shoulder: my right ear is grazed, and there's a hole in my thick hair. I've never been in a gang, never did a drug, never stole a chocolate bar. . . and I've been shot at three times—that's excluding the times Dad took a shot at me (the other times were in 6th grade while walking home, and in 7th grade on the playground). What did Ann Landers once write?. . . *shoot at me once, shame on you; shoot at me twice, why the hell don't you move out of L.A.; shoot at me three times, what the hell are you still doing here, MORON?!* With what I have in the bank, I figure I can go to Europe for a couple of months and meet people from around the world, shoot videotape, and stay in Youth Hostels for $10 a night (cheaper than a bachelor apartment).

I see Jonathan Miller's production of *Tristan und Isolde* at the Music Center. I write to Dr. Miller, asking if, for his upcoming production of *The Mikado* at the L.A. Opera, I can be a "dogsbody" (that's what Richard E. Grant did for Miller at the Donmar Warehouse when Grant first emigrated from Swaziland. I don't know what a dogsbody actually is, but presume it's dog-like work). Rats. . . I was planning to go to Europe, and Miller comes here!

I keep telling myself, "You're only 21—stop beating yourself up so much!" Then, moments later, my brain's other hemisphere retorts, "You're *21*—Orson Welles did *Citizen Kane* at 26—that's only five more years! At the rate you're going, you'll be lucky to get another *short* film made. Welles was doing *War of the Worlds* at your age! What are *you* doing? *Selling books*! You'll be hocking booze on t.v. *next year*!" I make a vow: I will have a film shown in a real movie theatre with a *real* audience (i.e. not a film festival audience) by the time I turn 26.

I must write another feature, a better one than *The Necessity of Being Frank*. It's tough to think of anything in a four-hour block of time. Just when my brain starts to whirl—time to go to work! I can't even come up with a concept. I *thought* I had at least one good idea in Professor's class, but I can't remember it. . .

CHAPTER 15

1988, Age 21

That Bergman Guy

Dudley's Rolls

Thanks to competition from conglomerates like Crown Books, Hunter's goes out of business. The phone rings at 6am on January 1st: Professor's friend tells me to vacate his apartment by noon tomorrow—he's lost his soap opera job in New York. Luckily, Mom has not made good on her threat to rent my room out to COLLEGE

STUDENTS, hardworking young people going to COLLEGE to get DEGREES, so I don't have to sleep in the Suicide Pinto this week. I would rather rough it in European youth hostels than in another bachelor apartment in L.A. I've saved enough money to last five months, having sunk to an all-time low on Christmas Eve: hawking copies of *Georgia O'Keeffe's 100 Flowers* on the streets of Beverly Hills to procrastinating yuppies for triple the $100 cover price.

The day before I leave for Frankfurt, I finally get a letter from Jonathan Miller, on his personal stationery. . . so I guess I have to take *this* rejection personally. "Dear Jürgen, I'm glad you enjoyed *Tristan und Isolde*, although it was really David Hockney's production, and I was simply a real-estate agent showing the singers around Hockney's set. . . " I keep scanning for the "Unfortunately. . . " or "I regret that I cannot. . . " line, and finally find at the end of the letter "You would be very welcome at *The Mikado* rehearsals. . . " (!)

I arrive two hours early at the rehearsal hall in downtown L.A. The stage manager, as usual, glares at me. Stage managers hate directing interns. *Hate them.* They think you're going to get in everyone's way, eat all the cookies (in my case, true), and write a best-selling book (in my case, also hopefully true). Jonathan Miller almost drops his cigarette when I introduce myself: he thought he was corresponding with a 6'4" male blonde UCLA Viking, but is greeted by a 5'4" female Celtic bottle-brunette high school dropout. Jonathan kicks off rehearsals by telling the Music Center Opera staff how much he loathes the Dorothy "Chandelier" Pavilion and Placido Domingo, the company's most beloved figure. The opera staff beams every time Jonathan derides their organization, much like people took delight in being insulted by Groucho Marx.

Speaking of Groucho, this production of *The Mikado* is heavily inspired by the Marx Brothers' film *Duck Soup*. Jonathan even shows the company a video of Groucho's grand entrance in the film, which he's replicating for Ko-Ko's entrance. Jonathan is impressed that I can sing along with *Hail, Freedonia*. The opera singers' skins crawl when they hear my voice, and I see them panicking: *What role is* she *singing?!* By knowing the Marx Brothers' music and how to correctly pronounce "nuclear," I've passed Jonathan's litmus test, and am not filed into the Dumb American category, phew.

Our Ko-Ko, Dudley Moore, makes his entrance, just hours after marrying his third wife in Las Vegas. He announces to all, "You're welcome to the consummation!" This *Mikado* is a revival of Jonathan's English National Opera production. Everyone has watched the BBC video of that production, and as they're copying it beat-for-beat, rehearsals are only two weeks long. It's not a very good learning experience, as I won't get to watch Jonathan create a show. He lets the assistant choreographer and assistant director do the majority of the slogging (he even flies off to Toronto for a few days in the middle of rehearsals). Jonathan often acts out scenes for the cast. I presume this is because they are singers first, not actors, and he uses this as a shorthand.

With everything already set in stone, if I manage to make one useful suggestion, I'll be surprised. An opportunity is presented within the first two hours. Rehearsing the opening chorus, singing, "We are gentlemen of Japan," Jonathan is doing a "comedy" bit where the obviously Caucasian chorus members put their fingers to the outer edges of their eyes and lift them, like the childish mimicking of Orientals. I scurry over to Jonathan and whisper, "Uh, excuse me, but, you *have* to cut that. It might go over in England, but here, you'll have picketers on opening night!" Jonathan blows smoke, literally (like most English doctors, he's a champion smoker), and he moves to another seat. I wait for him to get the stage manager to boot me out, but, luckily, Peter Hemmings (the Music Center Opera's General Director) comes in. Jonathan forgets about me and insults Hemmings's organization again. Hemmings beams, making mental notes so he can quote the quotable Jonathan at his next party.

After lunch, they rehearse the opening chorus again. Dudley, who has been preoccupied with his child bride and shooting *Arthur 2-On The Rocks*, sits in the auditorium learning his lines. He looks up, sees what the chorus is doing and sings out, "Uh, *Jon*-a-THAN! You can't do that *here*, or you'll have picketing!"

After that, Jonathan asks me on a regular basis if I like the bits he comes up with. The Assistant Director is bitchy and, like a film A.D., does all the yelling, whipping and bad guy stuff. Jonathan gets to come in with soothing tones and calm the fears. Jonathan's style: rehearse for a few minutes, then spend ten minutes telling stories about his other productions or explaining what he wants by making elaborate comparisons with art, literature, neurology and history ("See how BRILLIANT I am!"). Almost all of his references go right over everyone's head, but it's still entertaining. Sometimes Jonathan will tell a story that needs no references, so everyone in the cast can laugh out loud for real, not just act like, of course, they know what the hell Jonathan is talking about! (An example: Jonathan recently did *Long Day's Journey into Night* on Broadway, starring Jack Lemmon [and a hustling kid named Kevin Spacey]. Jonathan says he and Lemmon were walking down a street in New York when a drunk stumbled up to Lemmon and said, "Hey, Mr. Lemmon, can you help me out, I'd like to get a cup of coffee." Lemmon replied, "Coffee, *coffee*. . . look what it's doing to you!")

On opening night of *The Mikado* at the Wiltern (not the Dorothy "Chandelier"), Jack Lemmon sits in the row in front of me. Dom DeLuise sits next to me, crushing me with his girth, and promptly falls asleep. His nephew is in the politically corrected chorus, and whenever they finish a number, DeLuise wakes up and yells, "BRAVO!" At the end of Act One, DeLuise applauds with such big movements, he knocks me out of my seat. Jonathan has seen me literally rolling in the aisle, and cheerfully comments afterwards, as he autographs my *Beyond the Fringe* record album, "You fell out of your chair!"

Dudley signs my *Fringe* albums: "Dear Jürgen, Thank you for almost everything. Love, Dudley." Three *Fringe*rs down (Paxton signed the '64 album), Alan Bennett and Peter Cook to go. I ask Dudley, "Would you please fulfill another lifelong fantasy?"

Dudley leers and leans forward.

"Can I take your Rolls-Royce for a spin?"

I must get me one of these cars. It's like being back in the womb, but with a better stereo system. Dudley keeps one hand on the wheel and perspires. Driving four miles an hour around the Wiltern's parking lot, I tell him why he owes me this ride:

"Our Pinto was stolen when we drove it to see *Arthur*."

Dudley screeches, "You should *thank* me for that!"

Macbeth and Nessie's Neighbourhood

Mrs. Vincent takes me to my last decent meal before I go to food-free England. Her final words of advice for the young intellectual woman director? "Get a rich sugar daddy!" Armed with a copy of *Let's Go* (the budget travel guide written by Harvard students traveling with Daddy's American Express card), I arrive in London with $3,018. All the youth hostels are full, but I manage to find Earth's worst "B&B" (*Bunk Bed* [no breakfast]), with a co-ed toilet (the male guests have horrific aim—when standing *and* squatting). I may have gotten one of the film internships I applied for, but I will never know—Professor's friend has thrown away all my mail, and Australian drug dealers have monopolized the B&B's hallway phone.

I read in *Plays International* that Jonathan's next show is Leonard Bernstein's musical adaptation of Voltaire's *Candide* (Dick Cavett's theme music!), so I go to a bookstore to buy Voltaire's novel. As I approach the register, I hear a man say, "Good God. . . " I look up and see Jonathan Miller himself, dry-cleaning slung over his shoulder, paying for a stack of books. He looks at what I'm buying and says, "I'm directing that next week at Scottish Opera."

I say, "I know, that's why I'm buying it. Can I come up and watch rehearsals?"

"Certainly," Jonathan says, cracking his chewing gum. "See you there!" and he's off.

I race back to the B&B, grab my backpack, and run to Victoria Coach Station. I ask for a "ticket to Scotland."

"WHERE in Scotland?" the ticket seller barks.

I draw a blank. In typical Jonathan fashion, he's failed to mention that small detail. As the queue behind me grows impatient with the Loud Dumb American, images of Scottish culture flood my brain. . . *Macbeth*, The Loch Ness Monster, *Nancy Drew and the Clue of the Whistling Bagpipes*. . . all of which take place in the same locale. . . "Inverness?"

I climb aboard for the 12-hour journey. A woman who gets on in Lockerbie knows that Scottish Opera is in Glasgow (five stops before Inverness).

Scots Wha Hoo!

Glasgow is magnificent: the architecture, the people, the amount of sugar and grease. . . I'm in Scotland, *SCOTLAND!*—okay, now, be cool. . . act like a native. . . just waltz past those kilt shops with autographed photos of James "Scotty" Doohan's Canadian face in the windows. No Nessie souvenirs! And for God's sake, don't even mention *bagpipes!*

I arrive at Scottish Opera and meet my first Real-Live Scot, Robert Jones: practical, inventive, funny, and smoking even more than Jonathan. He confides that he's about to enter Assistant Director Hell—TWO directors! Which he didn't know about when he signed his contract with Scottish Opera, and he was only told yesterday, so it's too late to get out. An actor in *One-Way Pendulum* at the Old Vic Theatre (where Jonathan is the new Artistic Director) has fallen ill, and Jonathan needs go down to London to supervise the replacement (I wonder why Jonathan doesn't just have his A.D. break in the new actor?). John Wells, one of many, many writers working on the musical's book, who has no directing experience (although that's never stopped a man from getting the job), will take over while Jonathan is away. Hydra Time! I've brought my camcorder to rehearsals in the hopes of shooting my first documentary, but the Administrator takes one look at my camera and orders me to "REMOVE THAT!"

At the read/sing-through, Jonathan confidently announces to the quivering cast and crew, "John Wells and I speak as one person." Robert and I exchange looks and try not to groan audibly. There's nothing worse than being an assistant director sandwiched between two directors.

Amazing Nickolas Grace

When Jonathan attends *Candide* rehearsals, he acts out the roles for the actors. I thought he was doing this during *The Mikado* because there was so little rehearsal time, but this is his method (I wonder if he tried it with Gielgud and Olivier?). I see the veins in several actors' necks bulging, but they say nothing. When Nickolas Grace (Anthony Blanche from *Brideshead Revisited*) asks Jonathan, "Should I move stage left on this line?" Jonathan goes into a four-minute tirade against Sir Peter Hall, the National Theatre, and how every director (but him) thinks they're God. Nick listens closely, nods, and says, "That's brilliant. . . should I move stage left on this line?"

Back on his home soil, Jonathan's verbal attacks on Americans intensify, from "movie actors whose brains are not disturbed by a single thought," to that icon of PBS, Alistair Cooke, "the urologist who pushes the suppository of culture up the arsehole of America." I keep wondering when this lethal wit is going to be turned against *me*, and I spend more time figuring out how to avoid it than paying attention to what's going on in rehearsals.

Tension mounts as the script is rewritten every five minutes. Nick spends all night memorizing new pages, only to have them cut the next morning. I contribute to the paranoia by constantly writing in my journal during rehearsals, about a thousand pages in tiny paper-saving handwriting. Nick has the added burden of constantly having to tie my shoelaces, fix my collar, and lecture me on my appalling diet (I'm *presuming* he's no relation to Mr. Nickolas in Minnesota, the man who gave me my first film editing equipment). Most of all, everyone fears "Lenny" dropping in and ripping everything to shreds. It's Bernstein's 70th birthday year, and *Candide* is one of many world-wide celebrations. After weeks of apprehension, Bernstein comes to one of the final rehearsals. Luckily for us, Lenny just gives enormous compliments, makes a few excellent suggestions, and says he'll see us on Opening Night.

Candide sells out every performance and gets good reviews, but anything less than critics falling on their knees and crying "Genius!" and Jonathan gets depressed and dismisses the production as a folly. Jonathan goes home to London. I go hitchhiking in the Outer Hebrides, avoiding touristy places like Inverness and the Edinburgh Tattoo.

Jonathan lets me watch the taping at BBC-Scotland of Michael Ignatieff's *Dialogue in the Dark*, a conversation between David Hume and James Boswell. On the first day of taping, Jonathan announces, "Stephen Frears would insist this be done on film. Video is *just* as good." I reply, "I really like your lighting, but I'm with Frears—film is *way* better than video!" The Producer and Editor gasp at this up-start who dares contradict the director, and they order me to go fetch Jonathan cigarettes (great, I'm going to be responsible for giving Jonathan lung cancer, in addition to Gene Hackman's impending heart attack).

Young Director at Old Vic

For summertime fun at the Old Vic, Jonathan is directing (all by himself!) an obscure Jacobean tragedy, *Bussy D'Ambois*. I, however, am not all alone. I have a rival: Dick, another directing "observer." On the first day, when introducing himself, he tells all the actors he's the A.D. There is no actual A.D.; Jonathan only uses one when it's a big show. When the associate artistic director takes Dick aside and tells him to stop telling everyone that, Dick just grins at her. A month later, Dick applies to a theatre company that has a budget for an A.D. He writes on his C.V. that he was Jonathan's A.D., and he gets a P.J. (Paying Job)! Do I learn from the pro? *Nooooooo*, I continue to do any menial job that needs doing, and be obedient and "well-liked" by the actors, but with no official title or work permit. On the sly, I'm given £10 a week out of petty cash for making coffee and fetching sandwiches. Jonathan says I can be the A.D. for *King Lear* in January; they can get a work permit for me by then. I had enough money to survive for five months, and am now heading into my sixth month. I live off the Old Vic's tea and cookies and Jonathan's abandoned cheese sandwiches. I ask Jonathan if he'll take me to some parties (so I can make My Entrance in London Theatrical Society). Jonathan says he *never* goes to parties; he goes home and reads. So, in all those interviews, when he said he got directing gigs because people at parties asked him to direct, he was just telling stories? Like a dummy, I believed them.

Jonathan has a sudden burst of "inspiration" and decides to play Ennio Morricone's *The Good, The Bad, and the Ugly* theme as *Bussy D'Ambois*'s curtain-raising music. Jonathan asks me, "Isn't that good?" I've watched every single word I've said since February, but I'm tired and off my guard. I revert to my normal manner and blurt, "No, I hate it! The audience is going to laugh." Jonathan has the stage manager send me out for cigarettes. Later, Davy Cunningham (the lighting designer), tells me the S.M. *tactfully* talked Jonathan out of using the music. I don't realize till weeks later that Jonathan never asks my opinion again.

When Jonathan goes out of town, he lets me housesit, a nice change from sleeping in the Vic's costume storage. I watch a tape of his BBC film, *Alice in Wonderland*. It's a great film. It was made in 1966 (that finest of years), aired to loud protests, and was never seen again. Poor Jonathan will have to something radical to get it re-aired—direct a Hollywood blockbuster or, better still in the eyes of the BBC, die (it's often the best career move an artist can make). Alan Bennett, *Beyond the Fringe* #3, lives across the street from Jonathan. I want to knock on the door and say hello, but there's an old lady living in a van in his driveway who screams at me every time I even look at his house.

Dudley's Butler

Jonathan returns, and back into the costume bin I go. Across the street from the Vic, I see a nice old man trying unsuccessfully to flag down a taxi. With my Loud American voice, I start to yell "TAXI!" when I realize the nice old man is John Gielgud. I use the line that's opened many doors (and closed a few): "Hi, I'm apprenticing with Jonathan Miller at the Old Vic!" Gielgud asks me, "Are you learning many useful things? Have you ever been to Germany?" and "How much do you make at the Vic?" (the sallow look must give me away). I tell him, ten pounds a week. Gielgud says, "That's what *I* made when I started at the Vic! Of course, ten pounds a week went further in 1929, I suppose. . . "

When a taxi stops, I motion to the Vic and say, "Come on in! Everyone would love to see you." He says, "Oh, I don't want to bother them. . . " John (my, aren't we informal) opens the taxi door, gets in, and says, "When you're casting your next film, remember how nice I was to you!"

Dining with The Exorcist

The tension that greeted Leonard Bernstein's arrival at Scottish Opera pales in comparison with Max von Sydow's arrival at the Old Vic. Whereas Lenny descended for a few hours, posed for photos, French-kissed all the men and left, Max will be rehearsing for five weeks and playing for seven weeks. He's playing Prospero in *The Tempest* (another Miller revival—20 years after the first production. Same concept, same music). The production office carpet is vacuumed, dressing room Number One is painted, and the associate artistic director asks me, "You're Swedish, aren't you?" For the ten-thousandth time in my life, I'm about to reply, "No, German. . . " (*und I vas not responsible!*) But I stop as I open my big mouth, realizing a Swedish opportunity is coming, and blurt, "Yes—I mean, *Ja, Ja, Sverige! Jag har slagit av en tand!*" in an accent phonier than The

Muppets's Swedish Chef. Luckily, she buys it, and *Ja!*—I'm excused from Sandwich Detail, and assigned to run lines with Max von Sydow!

Max arrives. Jonathan stands up straight, but Max is taller. Everyone calls him *vaughn see-daw*. The not so-dumb American *vy-zick* pronounces it correctly: *fon sue-doff*. The Vic staff is acting English all of a sudden. Max gets to hear words like "Please" and "Thank you."

Assigning *me* to run Shakespearean lines with Max was moronic—me, an American who has only learned two Swedish swear words from her mother's high school exchange student's 10-year-old daughter. And, as Max started learning English in 1965, he's actually been speaking English longer than me (*than I?*). He also speaks French, German, Italian, and "dabbles" in Russian. Because he's played Prospero in Swedish, to keep from getting confused, he's speaking only English while in London. The only word I help Max with is *tortoise*. Max nails the iambic pentameter, and we spend our lunch hours actually eating lunch, in restaurants—*decent* restaurants! All the weight I've lost in the last seven months gets packed back on after just one week of Max's generosity. We walk to lunch in broad daylight, but, as this is restrained England, Max is not hounded by autograph seekers. . . although I see a lot of people stopping in their tracks and thinking, *Was that The Exorcist?*

Jonathan is constantly asking Max, "How did Bergman do this? What did Bergman say about that?" Max is always polite, but seems a little bored with the topic, and I'm confused. . . I can't remember *any* films Max did with Ingrid Bergman. And I don't recall reading that Ingrid directed anything. Jonathan grinds out his cigarettes when Max enters the room, never stands too close, and treats Max as though he might go off at any moment. Me? Hey—it's Max, the star of *Conan the Barbarian*! *Three Days of the Condor*! And J.C. Himself in *The Greatest Story Ever Told*! Of course, Jonathan never once mentions Max's forays into Hollywood. Max and I never once discuss theatre, only films, and Max seems thrilled when I tell him I was rooting for his Ming the Merciless to kill Flash Gordon. Thanks to my ushering stint at the Laemmle Theatres, I've also seen several obscure Danish films he starred in, like *Wolf at the Door*. I suspect Max views me as a breath of fresh air—he must be sick of being asked about what it was like to work with the star of *Casablanca*.

Max Baby

The following week, while running from the Underground guards for not having a valid ticket, it occurs to me that *Bergman* might, in fact, be Ing*mar*, the Scandinavian equivalent of Orson Welles; the morose Swedish dude who made nudie films my parents saw in college; the director Smoking Dick compared me to. My Bergman Theory gains momentum when I visit the Museum of the Moving Image. In one of the last exhibits, I see Max (Max is in a museum!). In a photo from a 1955 film, *The Seventh Seal*, Max is playing chess with Death (just like me and Dad!).

Unfortunately, the museum staff forcibly ejects me ten minutes after closing time, before I learn who directed the film. The next day during the final dress rehearsal, I tell Max I've figured out that *The*

Seventh Seal is a reference to the bible, not to aquatic mammals (even though the film takes place near the beach). He says I'm correct. I've also remembered the director worshipped by Woody Allen (with whom Max worked on *Hannah and Her Sisters*), and I ask Max, "Did you ever work with that Bergman guy?"

Max kindly replies to the young director, "A few times." Jonathan, overhearing, snorts his upper-middle-class nasal guffaw. With that one question, months of useful suggestions are wiped from memory, and I've officially flown into the Dumb American pigeonhole.

Coffee for Dr. Lecktor— Hold the Fava Beans

Much as I love watching Max, I keep thinking, *Why can't we just cut? And I'm sick to death of being in the same location for an hour!* Oh, God. . . it's time to face facts: I'm in the wrong media. I think cinematically, not theatrically. I don't know if my brain was hard-wired this way, or it's because, growing up, I saw fifty times more films than plays. Being In The Theatre, I also feel like a hypocrite. I can't afford to *go* to the theatre, so, what the hell am I doing working in it? Entertaining the upper classes? What about the scum (like me)? I decide to stick around until *King Lear*. The A.D. title will look good on my C.V. and it could lead to a P.J.

I overhear Jonathan saying he's going to a party for Peter Cook. . . a PARTY?! Jonathan has declined to introduce me to his "shy neighbor" Alan Bennett, but I want to meet at least one more Fringer. Jonathan tells me, "Cook is a drug addict. You don't want to go; he's not the Peter Cook you know from *Fringe*." I say I don't care; half a Cook is wittier than most people. But Jonathan leaves without telling me the address. I later kick myself—*Dick* would have followed him.

Next up, Jonathan directs a revival of his Royal Shakespeare Company production of *The Taming of the Shrew*. The RSC's home, the Barbican, is one of the true architectural horrors of the Western

World, so Petruchio and Kate come to the Vic's rehearsal room to work on their scenes. I nearly have a heart attack when Hannibal "The Cannibal" Lecktor (aka Brian Cox, aka Petruchio) from *Manhunter* asks me if it's too much trouble to make some coffee. Funny how, in real life, the cinema's greatest villains are sweethearts, and the romantic leading men, creeps. I whisper to the Stage Manager, "Is he Alan [Watson in *Young Sherlock Holmes*] Cox's dad?" The Stage Manager says, "Yes, but DON'T SAY THAT—he'll clobber you!" Fiona (Kate) Shaw drinks my brew and exclaims, "GoooOOOD coffee—you must be American!"

Beat it, Kid

The last Old Vic production of the season is the revival of Scottish Opera's *Candide*. Nickolas Grace resumes tying my shoelaces, fixing my collar and lecturing me on my appalling diet. The first week, Robert Jones directs (all by himself!) while Jonathan goes off to American on a lecture tour and makes fifty ten times more money than Robert. For Opening Night, I help Robert get into Highland Dress, with the help of a manual enclosed with the kilt rental (*wrap kilt apron around front as seen in Diagram K*). Robert answers an age-old question when, after fastening the kilt pin, his knickers come off: "Ah, that's better!" I ask why he didn't dress like this for Opening Night at Scottish Opera. He says he only feels patriotic when in England.

Jonathan may hate critics, but he loves giving interviews. As I sit in the production office writing notes about last night's show, a journalist asks Jonathan: who will he invite to direct other productions at the Vic next season? Jonathan says, "Well, I'm not hiring some 22-year-old!" As yesterday was my 22nd birthday, I start to get the hint. I stop writing, open the phone book, and look for the nearest travel agency. Jonathan then nails the hint into my forehead when he announces to the journalist that he's engaging Robert Jones as his Assistant Director for *King Lear*. Two days later, I fly back to L.A.

Hollywood (or Culver City), Here I Am

Mom has abandoned Auschwitz and moved in with Grandmother. Upon returning to Hell, my first act is to rip up our fucking ugly green carpeting. I haul it, and our revolting urine-colored sofa and the godddamned ugly lamps out to the curb. I sit on the bare wood floor and watch Max/Ingmar videos: *The Seventh Seal, Wild Strawberries, Through a Glass Darkly*, and *Winter Light*. Thank God I didn't know what classic films Max was in: I would either have been too tongue-tied to talk to him, or else, just another member of the "Bergman this, Bergman that" crowd.

At Christmas dinner, my great-uncle John asks what I was doing in England. I say, "I was Jonathan Miller's apprentice at the Old Vic, and—"

Uncle John drops his fork, and his salmon lands on the tablecloth. "*Dr.* Jonathan Miller?!?"

Uncle John turns to Mom and booms, "The *Old Vic*??! You never told me you had such a talented daughter! You said she was working in some rinky-dink summer stock company! I met *Dr.* Miller a few years ago, and he's the most intelligent man on the planet!"

I ask, "Can I have that piece of salmon, Uncle John?"

Because Uncle John is impressed, Mom is finally impressed, and I no longer have to fear being evicted from my room by COLLEGE STUDENTS. Now, all I have to do is come up with a no-budget feature screenplay. Although I can occasionally afford to go to films, I sure as hell can't afford to produce them.

CHAPTER 16

1989, Age 22

Fingerspitzengefühl

I Sucked Charlotte's Web Up My Vacuum Cleaner

While I was in the U.K., a friend taped the last twelve episodes of *Marblehead Manor* for me. The bastards stole *every* joke I wrote in my *Father of the Butler* episode. Great minds thinking alike? Hardly— the thieves. Should I sue? I have plenty of evidence. They should at least pay me *something*. But I don't want to ruin my reputation before I even have one, and man, those lawyer fees. . . !

I was forced to spend my entire childhood with Mom and Dad's drunken friends—no wonder I like to sit alone and just enjoy the quiet. But there isn't much at Auschwitz: the two unemployed spoiled brat grown sons living on either side of me (the same ones who Mom forced me to help with their stupid paper routes) are now on drugs, and they train their dogs to bark non-stop. I can't afford new furniture or paint, and no matter how many Rembrandt and John Singer Sargent posters I put up, the house is still Auschwitz. I would get a roommate if they were quiet and like Dr. Watson, but considering how decrepit this house is, I would only attract someone like Dr. Mengele.

Time to start squirreling away for the next film. Mom paid her maid $10 an hour, and she didn't even speak English. I would earn $3 an hour minding peoples' children, but can make more than three times that mopping their floors (people have interesting priorities).

I put up flyers in condo laundry rooms ("Recession Maid! Native English-Speaker Can Read Labels and Instructions, and Yes, *I Do Windows!*"). I place advertisements in Presbyterian newsletters, praying that Christians will be less likely to write bad checks or accuse me of stealing their silverware. My first job's first order: "Kill all the spiders!" *With the rich and mighty, always a little patience. . .* but come ON! I remind my employer, *If You Want to Live and Thrive, Let the Spider Stay Alive!* but she doesn't buy it. My second client executes the same order. (Idea: bring SNAKES into these womens' homes, and toughen up these little fraidy cats.) I escort the spiders outside, or relocate them to the far corners of walk-in closets and encourage them to hang out amongst the politically incorrect fur coats that my employers no longer dare wear in public but haven't the heart to give to the homeless.

I had noble visions of freeing working mums from housework to spend quality time playing educational games with their children, or giving hotshot lady doctors more time to find the cure for AIDS. Unfortunately, *those* women can't afford to hire me, and I work exclusively for childless women who think that a speck of dust = death. They apologize profusely for not having cleaned the house before my arrival. I mostly sterilize perfectly clean countertops, and turn shampoo bottles so the labels face outwards. . . christ, anything to make it look like I did *something*. When I leave, they exclaim, "Oh, it looks *so* much better now!" I have to force myself to stay in character, and remember to act like Gordon Jackson in *Upstairs, Downstairs*, or William Powell in *My Man Godfrey*, *not* like Paxton Whitehead and John Gielgud's sarcastic butlers.

The people I clean for on Saturday mornings have a magnificent booze collection. They're lucky I don't drink. But, one of their bottles catches my eye: MIDORI (named after the violinist, or *Ito*, the figure skater?). After a few weeks of just admiring the beautiful bottle from a distance, I take a teaspoon, pour out a sample, and taste it. *Yummy!* It's so *sweet!* I have another, and another, then I get a glass out and. . . wait a minute. . . what the FUCK am I doing!!!?! Man, I can't even say *nyet* to a second chocolate bar, I just keep eating them till I'm sick to my stomach. Phew, that was a close one. And what an expensive (not to mention, pretty ridiculous) drink to get hooked on.

Rotten Wroughten Film

I have to rebuild my film C.V. from scratch. I've never had any regrets before, but boy, do I regret going to screenwriting classes. I started Professor's class with good instincts, and came out a rule-abiding hack with writer's block. I'm also suffering from Directoritis: I've got to shoot *something* (with a camera, and something besides my stuffed animals); anything with a beginning, middle and end (and something I can make in a few days). I hunker down, and come up with a 12-page script about two girls competing for a music scholarship, with the flutist trying to kill the cellist. Phew, a relief, to finally get something down on paper! And it follows all of Professor's rules.

Location scouting in L.A. when you're over 8 years old is a nightmare; unless you're a gap-toothed kid making a school project ("Oh,

117

aren't you *precious!*"), all you hear is, "We charge $4,000 a day for a filming permit!" The Majors have spoiled it for the little guy; no wonder indy films are usually shot in parents' houses or in the desert. All I need is a small theatre with a piano, but every theatre in L.A. has realized you can make a fortune renting it out for a shoot. I do a quick rewrite, and now the music competition takes place in a church. But the Presbyterians have gone Hollywood (they want $600 a day!), so I convert to Methodism (did they invent The Method?). God will understand.

All my old crew have school loans to pay off, and full-time jobs, and shopping to do in the evenings and yard work on the weekends. I put up notices at AFI, UCLA, USC, high schools, and community colleges: "Director of 25 short films seeks Crew. No pay but short shoot, copy of film, food, and Fun, Fun, Fun!" I get only one reply, from an American Film Institute "Director of Photography" (I think the title *Cinematographer* is more elegant, but he insists on *D.P.*). I draw up a budget: $1,100. The D.P. says no, the script is *so* good, we've *got* to shoot it on 3/4" tape. He knows where to rent a camera for $1,100 (there goes the whole budget). For the exteriors, Pomona College waives their usual $5,000 per day fee, but demands I be heavily insured. There goes another $400.

Goodbye, Rommel. . . Hello, Goebbels!

On the first day of shooting, Laurence Olivier dies—not an encouraging sign. The D.P.'s idea of complimenting me is saying how much he admires the Nazis for "taking control" of Europe. Do I listen to my gut and FIRE this sick MOTHERFUCKER? *Noooooo,* I'm so desperate to shoot a movie, and he was the only person who answered my advertisement. He mocks me when I say "Please" and "thank you": "Oh, *yes,* madam!" Anytime I'm not smiling, he says, "Why are you so irritable? Is it that time of the month?" On the second-to-last day, as all the gentlemanly techniques Paxton and Jonathan Miller used for gaining co-operation haven't worked, I start shouting at him, like a stereotypical Movie Director, treating him with contempt and saying things that would make Jed Harris cringe— and he instantly bucks up! (What the hell is the AFI teaching their students?!)

I finish the movie. Congratulations, Vsych. . . on your first flop! I was so eager to get back into film (or even video), I neglected to notice one small detail: my script *sucked*. Nice going! I shove the master copy in a drawer and hope video deteriorates faster than nitrate film.

I see the restored version of *Lawrence of Arabia*. It's My Favorite Film. My second favorite is *Bridge on the River Kwai*, and third, *La Grande Illusion* (bumping *Jaws* to #4). I want to make a film like those—a great action film where I actually care about what happens to the characters. Much as I would kill, murder. . . nay, *slay!*—to make an epic, I don't dare dream bigger than $1m. Maybe someday.

"We're Number Three!"   "Damn those Limeys!"

1990—Age 23

New Year's Resolution: Never make a film unless the script is good. Like, *duh*! I knew that in nursery school. How the hell did I forget that?

Since George Bush has ignored my onslaught of anti-war postcards, I am ignoring his little war in the Gulf. I disconnect the t.v. antenna and watch tons of classic movies on video.

I'm going to leave La La Land. My brain is coagulating here. Before I die, it'd be nice to live someplace I actually liked. I want to go somewhere cultured and historic, where art isn't a dirty word, and make a film there. No one in L.A. wants to make anything smaller than a $5 million dumb teen comedy that will "launch their careers." I've never once heard one of my peers say anything like, "I want to make a great film," but I constantly hear, *I want a three-picture deal!* I'd better escape before my tender young mind gets infected by this crass commercialism. But where should I go? Someplace with access to film equipment, but where the locals aren't yet jaded about yet another film crew blocking traffic. Australia? Japan? Torrance? I could rent out Auschwitz, stay in a tiny room somewhere and live off the rental income. But first, I have to fix the electricity, plumbing, the lawn, the roof, replaster, and get rid of that hideous orange paint.

Arch d'Triumph!

Might as well get a screenplay out of my time with Professor—not by using his writing methods, but by writing a fictionalized account of our battles. . . how 'bout a black comedy about a writing professor who kills his prime student? Yeah!

Before I dive into writing screenplay #4, I go to the Nuart to see *Sunset Boulevard* and *2001: A Space Odyssey*. I am really surprised: both are considered classics, and yet they're so original, offbeat, and downright bizarre. Today, those scripts wouldn't even get past the D-Girls. I hope those films will help me to forget Professor's goddamned rules and just try anything. I want my *fingerspitzengefühl* back!

I watch *Comfort and Joy*, a great comedy about ice cream-truck wars in Glasgow. I love Bill Paterson. . . he could play Professor! What about moving to *Glasgow*? WOW! I speak the language (sort of), it has good writing weather, and the people are funny and smart (so much so, I might actually want to leave my room and maybe even talk to some of them). Glasgow has good public transportation, free museums, the Mitchell Library. . . *I'M GOING!* I'm a little worried that Paterson and the majority of Scottish actors are based in London, but London's just L.A. with higher prices and more cultured accents.

It's broiling hot in Auschwitz, and the psychotic neighbors and their dogs never shut up. I find sanctuary and write *Professor Oppressor* in the air-conditioned basement of the UCLA library (where Ray Bradbury wrote *Fahrenheit 451*). The library vibes are good, and I finish the first draft in only three weeks—back to my old self! And writing's not *that* difficult—what was Professor's problem? Lack of talent? Too much pressure by his wife to make money? Playing with his dog too much? *Professor Oppressor* has lots of black humor, but it's definitely going to be classified as a drama. Oy vey. Bergman (Ingmar) had to wait until he had a big box office comedy hit before he got financing for *The Seventh Seal* (of course, that "light comedy" was *Smiles of a Summer Night*—not exactly *Animal House*). I re-title my screenplay *Arch* (based the professor's character name and temperament). It needs a lot of polishing, and it's a little fatty.

I Should Have Taken Away Gene Hackman's Popcorn!

I initially advertised myself as "Recession Maid," then "American Maid," but after two years on the job and analyzing the demographics of my best customers, I now tout myself as "Bachelor Maid." Bachelors give tips and are much easier to please: fold the laundry, run the dishwasher, scrape the fossilized dog poop off the carpets and they're happy.

Gene Hackman has chest pains and has to be treated for a narrowing artery! Luckily, he's going to be okay, but he has to slow down and only make ten films a year. See what happens when actors don't listen to the director?

One day at a Time, Seize the day. . . For much of my life, the present has been unbearable. I've spent my whole life living in the future. Auntie Mame's *Live, live, live!* credo is hard. Things will be better when I go to Scotland. Margaret Thatcher finally got kicked out, just in time for my arrival (I hate her even more than Ronald Reagan—a woman *should* know better).

CHAPTER 17

1991, Age 24

Beam Me Up, Scotty

Go East, Young Woman

My rewrites improve *Arch*, but it's totally unpitchable ("It's *Apocalypse Now!* meets *Educating Rita!*"). I'll never get it funded in Hollywood. Can't wait to get out of here and see if my brain works better. It will also be a blessing to escape the crazy boy neighbors, who have taken to phoning me in middle of night and hissing, "We're going to kill you. . . and your *cat!*" I'm worried that I'm worried about my cat, but not myself.

I put my cat up for adoption, and fly to London. In Victoria Station, Sylvester McCoy (a Glaswegian and the current *Dr. Who*) knocks me down and steps on my hand. The day I arrive in Glasgow, Bill Douglas, the Ingmar Bergman of Scotland, dies. The following day, Blackcat Studios, Scotland's biggest sound stage, goes bankrupt. Are these three *signs*, or merely three *tests* of my resolve?

Moving from Hollywood to Glasgow is like escaping from Mordor and returning to the Shire! In keeping with total immersion in Scotland, I read Katherine Hepburn's autobiography *Me* (well, she did play *Mary Queen of Scots*). Hepburn got her first acting job by following her Dad's advice: "If you want something, don't call, don't write. Be there. In person. Harder to turn down a living person." Seems to have worked for Kate. I read that Hanif Kureshi popped *My Beautiful Laundrette*'s screenplay through Stephen Frears's mail slot, but that could just be another bullshit Show Biz Story.

The next day, the *Glasgow Herald* says Bill Paterson is starring with Juliet Stevenson in the world premiere of *Death and the Maiden* at the Royal Court Theatre Upstairs. I do a half-Hepburn/half-Kureshi and mail Paterson *Arch* with a letter warning him that I'm coming to London to see him and the show. How nice, to mail life-altering documents and know they'll actually get delivered—Rule, Royal Mail! I want to work with Paterson because he works with great scripts. Hope he'll think mine is one of them.

Bill double takes when I introduce myself: "I was expecting a man!" He looks off to the side and says, "I don't have the weight to get a film going. . . I can help get something on at the Royal Court Theatre Upstairs, but not £1 million film, you understand!" He asks me to meet him at the stage door in two days, after he's read my script. Bill is easy to talk to; I don't have to try to impress him to get him to listen to me, and his eye doesn't do that Hollywood wander around to see if there's someone more important nearby.

On the day, Bill is a no-show, feigning a headache, but he leaves a note asking me to phone him at home the next morning (if *Arch* was as good as *Lawrence of Arabia*'s screenplay, it would have cured any headache). Paterson talks to me until my coins run out. He says to change the young writer to a painter or photographer, or it'll put off the Scottish Production Fund: "Writers writing about writing is almost incestuous! And they get so many scripts like that." He also suggests trimming the dialogue; "It doesn't look like it's that much on the page, but you'll find it's a lot of screen minutes." He apologizes for sounding negative, and says if I get funding, "I'll do it." He likes the energy and characters, especially Ita, "She's great." Unlike Professor's red-penned comments ("WEAK—IMPROVE"), Bill's suggestions are actually useful and easy to implement.

Back to Glasgow. I've never been out at night: I'm always writing in my journal, polishing *Arch*, storyboarding, or watching unedited movies on Channel Four. When I venture out to see a Friday night play at the Tron, I finally witness the famed drunkenness—girls draping themselves over guys they wouldn't speak to if sober, men actually lying in gutters, and lakes of vomit (sorry, *lochs*) on the sidewalks (sorry, *pavement*).

I take the bus to the Edinburgh Fringe Festival and hook up with Howard Goorney, an actor from *Candide*, who treats me to a vegetarian meal and a lecture about my appalling diet. The vegetarian stuff tastes pretty good. Vegetarianism would really annoy the hell out of my landlord (he hates Gandhi), but I don't know how to start; how do you do without meat (macaroni and cheese?)? So I start reading labels and just stop buying stuff that has artificial flavours, colorings and preservatives (there goes 90% of my diet).

"*What* have the Romans Done for Us?!"

In September, I get my first letter. . . from the Head (sorry—*Heid*) of the Scottish Production Fund, who has the authority to allot bursaries. . . to arrange a meeting! (In Scotland, Mail, Good!) She wouldn't be inviting me in to reject me! She probably just needs my checking account information for the deposit.

When I arrive at 10:00am, the Heid is hung over—and *Arch* is about how alcoholic parents nearly destroy the life of Ita, a young woman painter (née writer). The Heid explains that the Fund only gives £5-10,000 bursaries to writers who have a treatment but no script. I say, "Huh? Don't you mean it the other way round?" The Heid says no: "They're for people who haven't actually written anything, to see if they have the slightest idea how to write dialogue or construct a screenplay. When a script is at the level yours is, we want to see a producer attached. . . so you don't fall neatly into any of the established categories." (Fuck *neatness*, I'll squeeze uncomfortably into £5,000!) She calls my script "an extraordinary piece of work and the strongest writing we've seen in years. . . *but*. . . " she goes on to blast all my script's best points, the ones Bill Paterson liked—especially Ita's character (Ita's in every frame. How she can like the script and hate Ita. . . ?). The Heid finishes her rejection by proclaiming, "And to top it off, there are *no* British films made about women!"

"Huh? Uh. . . huh?"

"Name *one* British film in the last ten years with a female lead that was successful."

"*Truly Madly Deeply!*"

"That was made for television, and only it was only shown in theatres because Alan Rickman was in *Robin Hood*."

I gently correct the pickle head, "Uh, *Robin Hood* was released AFTER *Truly Madly Deeply. . . The Lonely Passion of Judith Hearne, Shirley Valentine, High Hopes, Dance with a Stranger, Room with a View, The Dressmaker, Personal Services. . . "*

The Heid lights another cigarette and barks at her assistant to bring coffee.

"*. . . Wish You Were Here, Rita Sue and Bob Too, Blonde Fist, Breaking Glass, December Bride, Business as Usual. . .* and there are two

films coming out soon, *Antonia and Jane*, and *Enchanted April*—
that one stars FOUR women!—and oh! Oh—*Educating Rita*!"

The Heid exhales smoke like a volcano. "That wasn't a hit in the
States."

"Well, compared with *Star Wars*, it wasn't. . . *Letter to Brezhnev*,
Life is Sweet. . . christ, I can't think of that many recent *American*
films starring women—"

The Heid rolls her eyes. "But *apart* from those films, there are *no*
British films made starring women!" I feel like I've fallen into that
scene from Monty Python's *Life of Brian* where John Cleese argues,
"Apart from better sanitation, medicine, education, irrigation, public health, roads, freshwater system, baths and public order, *what*
have the Romans done for us?!"

The Heid says again, "Well, it's the best script we've had in a long
time, BUT. . . " I have to bite my lip to keep from blurting, ". . . *but
I'm a drunk and I'm not going to risk exposing myself!*" Well, now I
don't feel so bad. . . Americans aren't the only morons in the world.

My Ain Folk

I spend every morning in the Mitchell Library reading newspapers
with the swarms of unemployed men. I ask the Librarian (who knows
everything), "How do I meet people in Glasgow who would like to
make a film?" She says, "Och, the Glasgow Film and Video Workshop!" The GFVW is in a building with falling plaster and a roof
that leaks when it rains (i.e. five times a day). They're nice folks who
can't believe I left Hollywood to come here ("You've got it backwards!"). They have some of BBC-Scotland's old equipment: a 16mm
Arriflex camera that usually works, a Nagra, and a Steenbeck with a
flickering bulb.

The GFVW gets funding from the Strathclyde Regional Council
for Production Grants to make ten short films, and announces a
competition for short film projects. Think fast, Vsych! I strain for
ideas. . . how about this: *Wild Raspberries*. Paxton and I drive from

Inverness to Glasgow. Max von Sydow pumps us gas (uh, *petrol*). We give Ingmar Bergman and Sven Nykvist a lift, but throw them out after ten miles when they will not stop fighting about lenses. We see Martin Scorsese with his thumb out but, remembering his cameo in *Taxi Driver*, zoom past him. . . oy vey. I need to get out and meet *people*, or all my films are going to be about other films.

I keep my eyes out for Glaswegian eccentricities that I can spin into a story (I'll have plenty to choose from). I get a great idea for a Western—with Luigi Boccherini music.

Yee-*HAW!*

Man, I am never happy where I am. I wrote Glaswegian *Arch* in L.A., and now I'm going to write a Western in Glasgow. And Westerns are totally dead in Hollywood. Great timing!

I notice that formal yard sales (sorry, *jumble sales*) are rare here. People usually just place things they want to sell in their front windows and make a placard. As I walk down the Great Western Road, I see three houses in a row that have advertisements. "Bird for Sale: *Cheep!*" In the next window, there's a rocking chair for sale. Then a pram. In the fourth house, I see a sad little boy looking out the window, looking like no one wants him, as though there's a sign hanging above him reading, "Son for Sale." Ten years ago, one of my friend's fathers got really plastered at her Bats Mitzvah and woefully confided to me, "If I didn't have Sasha, I could have had a 46-foot yacht!" What if a father decided he'd *really* rather have a yacht than support his son, and he put the son up for sale? I write the script in four days, title it *Son for Sail* and deliver it to the GFVW.

For Christmas, just for fun, I try to write a film in one weekend. I can't think of any ideas for features, and my Western is not jelling, so I come up with a short film called *Pay Your Rent, Beethoven*. Beethoven is trying to compose, but he's been dumped by his last four girlfriends, so he's not been inspired to write anything memorable (or profitable). When he doesn't pay his rent on time, his landlord chases him around the house with a knife (it no doubt happened!). Beethoven is rescued by his neighbor Elise, who wears a fur coat (when I was a 6-year-old piano student, I thought *Fur Elise* referred to Beethoven's girlfriend's wardrobe). My script is a classical music variation on "You Must Pay the Rent!" "I Can't Pay the Rent!" "I'll Pay the Rent!" "My Hero!" I send the script to nice Pauline at the GFVW with a note saying, "Just wanted to give you a laugh."

On New Year's Eve, near Glasgow Cross, *finally*, I see a guy wearing a kilt: he looks GREAT! Everyone stares at him (even more so than if this were L.A.), like, *Who does he think HE is?* This is the first time I realize, "I'm in Nancy Drew's *Clue of the Whistling Bagpipes* Scotland—SCOTLAND!" I've only heard the pipes once since I came here. During the Edinburgh Festival, there was a guy playing outside the train station. He was a good photo opportunity. . . but the *noise*—BLAH!

CHAPTER 18

1992, Age 25

I Beat Orson Welles by 61 Days

The Scottish Production Fund Heid quits to go ruin some other organization, so I submit *Arch* to the new Heid. Apparently, the old Heid hated *every* script she got (rats—I thought I was special!). The new Heid puts *Arch* at the bottom of the sludge pile because I'm a "single writer"—meaning married to no agent or production company. The William Morris Agency in London asked to read *Arch*, but I've not heard back from them. Did the agent die? (A warm thought!)

Pauline at the GFVW writes (Good?) and says I've won a Production Grant—for 16mm!!—for *Pay Your Rent, Beethoven*!!!? I get to use whatever equipment of theirs is working at the time, plus up to five rolls of whatever raw film stock happens to be in their fridge at the time, and £100 for miscellaneous production expenses, like props and the all-important tea and biscuits (if I want an optical print, I'll have to pay for it myself). I call to make sure Pauline got the name of the film right. She says yes: "The consensus was that *Son for Sail* would be too expensive, and too complicated and difficult to make." (That opening scene with the yacht really scared them, I bet.) Pauline also says everyone "really disliked" the character of the son. Robert Jones, the A.D. from *Candide*, *was* interested in working on *Son for Sail*, but balked because he wasn't "terribly keen" about the son, either (American translation: *Yuck!*). Whaaaaa?! Sorry, kids, you're *wrong.* Pauline is impressed that I have screenplay and storyboards. The other filmmakers submitted treatments, and are going to wing it on the set—they turn up their noses up at "narrative" films, knowing experimental is the only *real* art form.

On the Friday afternoon before we start shooting, I go to pick up the raw film stock at GFVW. The film that happens to be in their fridge at the time is eight years old and has milk spilled on the can (*tin?* WHATEVER!). Pauline assures me that the film is fine. It's 4.45pm and no place in London can ship film in time for us to start shooting. . . I take a taxi to BBC-Scotland, burst through the doors and cry, "I need film, FILM! Help me. . . *heeeeeellllp meeeeeeee!*" sounding like the tiny guy trapped in the spider's web in *The Fly.* A man in a suit comes over, listens to my sad story, and says, "You're the one who said to Jonathan Miller, 'Film is better than video.'" Oh, FUCK. . . ! I admit it was me. He tells me to wait there. He returns carrying ten cans of film (fresh from Kodak! *I love the smell of freshly-canned film in the evening!*). I ask "How much?" He plops it in my arms and says, "Go make a masterpiece!"

Fur Coat Elise

Scottish Opera lets us shoot in the hall where *Candide* rehearsed. Our D.P. can't even follow directions to the location, and for some weird reason, he freaks out over shots that last longer than five seconds. On the last day, whenever we need a second take, the D.P. keeps saying, "Looked good to ME!" and I keep saying "No, we're going again!" He then says, "We're out of film!" and starts packing up. *What?!* I open a bag in the corner, and find another can. The D.P. throws his leather jacket across the room and storms out. Luckily, I've read the Arriflex manual and know how to load the film, so I pop off the last shot—a close-up of the *Für Elise* music.

| Method Director | Method Crew |

I have to wait ten days to see the footage: after Technicolour finishes their full-priced gigs, they then process the GFVW's film (someday, I'm going to have "dailies"). I get the rushes and start synching the picture and sound with an assistant editor who wants to move up to Editor. After twenty minutes of work, the GFVW's editing equipment explodes (*Pay Your Rent, Beethoven—a film so explosive, the Steenbeck couldn't handle it!*), so we sneak into Scottish Television at lunchtime, telling the guard we're working on *Taggart*, Scotland's biggest cop show.

I usually love watching the rushes. . . but what the !@#%^&*| ()_+|}{"?!! On *PYR,B*'s magnetic soundtrack, you hear our D.P. yelling "Speed!" and then I call "ACTION" and *then*, anywhere from 2-5 seconds later, the camera finally starts rolling. Then the camera cuts, and 2-3 seconds later you hear me yell "CUT!" What the !¢&¨$¹%Æ£#FUCÄ§Ï´¬ö¿Œ§¶Ä©!?

Taggart's head editor bursts in on us, but when she sees the rushes, she says, "They look good. . . carry on!" I can't afford to get an answerprint with an optical track, so I want to keep the workprint clean. The Glasgow Film Theatre (where the GFVW shorts will début) has a double-locking projector. My editor refuses to wear gloves, and constantly scratches the film. Scottish Television's joiner is defective (it's worse than Dad's toenail clippers!), so the film leaps at every single edit, making it very hard to gauge the comic timing. My editor disappears for five days, then telephones (Good) and says she and her boyfriend got back together, so she has to quit the film (Good!): she has to get a paying job so she can afford to buy new clothes and go to the salon so she'll be presentable enough to go out with him. So, bimbos are an international occurrence. With women like that in the industry, no wonder no one takes us seriously. I try cutting on my own, but my hands are killing me and they can't move as fast as my brain. I ring the editors listed in *Film Bang* and only have to get as far as the B's to find Bob Bathgate, a retired editor from BBC-Scotland who has one of Auntie Beeb's old flatbed Steenbecks. He likes our footage—especially my whip-pans (my favorite shot—I try to do one in every film). He agrees to work for free, but only from 11pm-2am (when I'm usually deep in my REM cycle). Bob assures me, no, I'm *not* crazy, and yes, my D.P. *is* Satan and was starting and stopping the camera whenever he felt like it. Bob patches up mistakes and shows me how, next time, I can improve cuts, "when you find a D.P. who takes directions!" It's like free night school.

The GFVW arranges a free mix at Scottish Television. Our mixer, Cy Jack, has thousands of effects, and we play with them for eight hours. If only I had known beforehand, I would have designed a more elaborate soundtrack! Mixing with a real sound editor is so much fun. I've come a long way since the times I tried to synchronize a tape recorder with my Super-8 films.

My Grandmother writes, asking, just what the hell am I doing with my life? She's a big lover of the arts (but—just my luck—not of films). I write back and explain what a film director does. She sends me a thousand bucks—post funding! It's almost enough to get an answerprint, with an optical track!

PH I L A N T H R
q 0

"Someday my Prince will come
And give my film a nice big sum
Oh, how thrilling that moment will be -
Auf Wiedersehen bankruptcy!
My landlord will smile
And not evict me for awhile
When my Prince's cheque finally clears!"

Charming Prince Charles sent me a cheque for £300 today! I applied for a grant from his foundation for young (under 26) entrepreneurs, The Prince's Trust. My first step towards getting a Royal Command Performance! It's my first grant ever, which goes straight to Technicolour for the optical track. I want to photocopy the historic document (the cheque), but I can't afford the 10p.

I find a calligrapher to make the film's titles. He shows me a great portfolio, but then falls into a month-long drunken stupor and does a hideous job. The only name you can read is mine, "and that's all that matters!" he burps. My crew is furious at me.

A Dog Ate My Film

My films have been in 25 film fests, but I've never gone with them (it was always a choice between go, or use the money to make another film). This will be the first time since *Tyrannosaurus Tex* that I've seen one of my films with an audience—and a foreign one, at that. There's no dialogue in *Beethoven*, so I hope it will travel around the world easily.

On Paxton Whitehead's birthday (October 17th), *Pay Your Rent, Beethoven* premieres at the Glasgow Film Theatre (Glasgow's version of the Nuart Theatre), screening in A Real Movie Theatre for A Real Audience Before I Turn 26 (I made my goal, with 61 days to spare!). It's a hit! Even though the theatre has only 220 seats, it's my biggest movie screen ever—much bigger than our livingroom wall. The audience HOWLS, and they don't even know me. Whoa! Aileen Ritchie's film doesn't have an optical track, and the projectionist can't get the film in sync, so her film is not shown. Prince Charles and my Grandmother saved my film's ass! My film is the third shown out of the ten. Everyone likes it, except my D.P. (of course), and seven of the other filmmakers, who attack me for having a story and "pandering to the audience" (they say films are to "express oneself"). I telephoned newspaper editors, but they sent their critics to *Beethoven*, the children's film about a dog, playing around the corner at the Cannon multiplex! The Glasgow Film Theatre screening sells out, and the manager programmes another screening in their big theatre.

It's hard to get people in the film industry into a movie theatre ("I want to see a tape!"), especially for "just" a short film. This is the first film of mine that I *want* to show everyone. I send out as many videotapes as I can afford to. The new Heid of the Production Fund loves *Pay Your Rent, Beethoven*. Of course, next month, she's quitting the business to have a baby, so sorry, she can't help me. I get a meeting in Edinburgh with a producer. I journey across Scotland (thank God it's a narrow country) so she can tell me her male partners turned down *Son for Sail* (they suddenly lost interest when they discovered the director wasn't male). On the bus back, I break out in hives for the first time in my life. The doctor says I'm having an allergic reaction to something. The next five producers I meet to discuss *Arch* pressure me to let "someone else" direct it (although they never once mention who that someone else might be. I wish the big chickens would just come out and say, "some *man*"). A week after I stop meeting these people, my hives go away, surprise, surprise.

I finally find a producer for *Son for Sail*. She doesn't like *Arch* or *Pay Your Rent, Beethoven* at all. Weird. . . I thought all my films would appeal to the same people, but people either hate *Arch* but love *Son for Sail*, or hate *SfS* but love *PYR,B*. The Producer says we'll apply to "First Reels," "Short and Curlies," and the British Film Institute's "New Directors" programmes. I draw up a £14,000 budget. My producer makes up one for £20,000 that slashes the crew's pay but gives her an 800% raise.

Pay Your Rent, Beethoven screens at the Edinburgh Fringe Film & Video Festival, and gets a great response from the dour Edinburghers! I resume research on my Beethoven feature screenplay. There's so much material on Beethoven, I could do a 13-hour miniseries! Should I make it a wild comedy, like the short? Then, I could peddle the short and say it's a demo for the feature (Hollywood loves that kind of thing; no one there can read, or has any imagination).

The Wrath of Vsych

I go to a salon and ask for "just a trim." Blind without my glasses, I can only see them sweeping up my hair the moment it hits the floor. They stick me under a dryer and run to lunch, saying I can let myself out. When I put my glasses back on, I see they've "trimmed" off twelve inches (and sold it?).

The Glasgow Film Theatre shows the GFVW's short films again, moving *Pay Your Rent, Beethoven* to top of the bill. Alas, nine-tenths of audience walks out before my film screens. But the GFT door-man tells me every person who made it to the bitter end came out saying, "The Beethoven film was the best!" The GFT later screens *PYR,B* before *Delicatessen* and *Slacker*, and pays me £27—my share of the box office receipts! I'm a Real-Live Filmmaker—with gross points!!

I go to the movies on my birthday, and the GFT charges me full Adult admission; my Young Scot card has expired. I'm 26 now—

Fun's Over! Society says it's time to stop fooling around and get a full-time job! For my last youthful fling, I convince Scottish Citylink to give me a few weeks grace and let me pay the Youth fare to my original 1988 destination, Inverness. I go on an old drunk's Volkswagen van Official Loch Ness tour. The loch is beautiful, but creepy: trees float in the black water, the light changes every ten seconds, and the wind makes waves that look like Nessies. One of the Orkney kids on the Volkswagen tour says to me, "You're the first American I've ever met!" I've heard that about five times since I moved here, and it dawns on me, *I'm probably the first Real-Live American most Scots have ever met.* Christ, that's a scary thought. Damn it, I should have been on my best behaviour!

My landlord's Mum kindly invites me to Christmas dinner. When I appear in the livingroom, my landlord is horrified that one of his tenants has dared set foot in his Christmas world, and he whisks me out; "Christmas is for FAMILIES." I'm hungry and, unlike heretical California, there's nothing open on Christmas. Well, it *is* Christmas . . . time to write another film! Gotta pick a topic, something I *hate*, something to fuel the flames. Besides my landlord, what has enraged me lately? *That hair salon!* A man bursts into the salon with a hair dryer in his holster, and blows the owner away!

Despite climbing two more steps up the ladder, my boyfriend dumps me for "someone who isn't spending all her time fiddling around with some hobby that, if it hasn't led to anything by now, isn't *going* to." Strange, how the whole world opens up to you after breaking up with a man. You can go anywhere! Think anything! Dress in clothes that make breathing painless! Eat enough food to keep brain cells functioning! Live longer now that you're no longer being used as a waste-basket for his emotional debris! And there's more time for movie-going—time previously wasted trying to undo all the damage his aloof father inflicted! I'm going to be famous and gets lots of presents and flowers and stuffed toy animals and he'll be sorry, sorry, sorry!

CHAPTER 19

1993, Age 26

Sun for Sale

Visiting Nessie's lair was inspiring, although I can't exactly see her influence on my new script. I write *Curl Up and Dye* in 18 days. Now, *that's* more like it. I read it, re-read it, and re-re-read it. . . nope, doesn't need any rewriting; I hit this one out of the ballpark! I guess it's my reward for slaving through *Arch*. I can even pitch it: *A mysterious drifter comes to a small Western town and saves it from its evil hair salon.* I was able to weave a lot of my Western-with-Boccherini-music ideas into *Curl Up and Dye*. It's my first flat-out comedy feature in years. Let's hope the Dark Decade is over.

"Tartan Shorts," another showcase for wee filmmakers, has a screening. One of the shorts is directed by my D.P. from *Pay Your Rent, Beethoven*. Why has he never boasted about his short to me? Is he embarrassed by his non-narrative snoozefest? Then, it hits me. In the lobby afterwards, I grin at him, showing all my teeth, and say loudly, "Where'd ye get yer *film?*" He slithers away. At last, I know the reason for his bizarre behaviour on *PYR,B*: he was stealing every frame of my film for *his* film!

When I fail to win any grants for *Son for Sail* (I'm too old to hit Prince Charles up for more dough), my producer pulls out, unwilling to "exhaust her connections" for "just" a short film (quitter!). *Curl Up and Dye* is set in the American West, and no place in Scotland can double for it. I could shoot both *SfS* and *Curl Up and Dye* in and around L.A. County... or, should I try New York again? It's a cheaper flight from Glasgow... but the only way I could afford to live there would be to move into another boarding house. I know a woman should be content with a room of one's own, but I really need a kitchen and no roommates with blaring stereos.

As I walk towards the aeroplane... I mean, *airplane* (gotta learn to talk American again), I have An Epiphany—*I shall return... a feature director!* I also have the feeling that I'm not going to see Scotland for a long, long time... maybe I should revise my epiphany. I don't want to make it *too* specific, or I may never get back! Well, I made my goal to get a film shown in a real theatre with a real audience before I turned 26... more importantly, a film I'm proud to show. Okay, it wasn't a feature, I forgot to spell out *that* small detail. Now, I want to make *$on for Sail*, and then *Arch* (I suspect whatever Beethoven script I come up with will be too expensive for a feature début, unless it's Beethoven terrorizing a lot of non-Screen Actors Guild teenagers in a haunted house [*The Corpse of Beethoven!*]).

I fly to Bonn and spend two days in the Beethoven House, getting ideas for my feature. The Heiligenstadt Testament (a suicide note in which Beethoven, mid-way through writing it, changes his mind about chucking it all) has to be the highlight of my film. The museum has brochures in Japanese... I remember reading that the Japanese *love* Beethoven's 9th Symphony. They even have huge sing-alongs with thousands of people (the Japanese really know how to party). . . how 'bout this: *Beethoven Ichi Ban Samurai!*

On the plane to L.A., I write an American version of *Arch*, set in Seattle (I'd rather shoot there than L.A.). My goal is to shoot *$on for Sail* in November, when production is usually slow, crew and actors are bored and need Christmas cash, vendors need to get their equipment off the shelves, and the sun is low on the horizon (shorter shooting days, but *great* light!). *$on for Sail* will cost a lot more to make in L.A. than in Glasgow—no one is going to work for free, and SAG minimum wages are terrifying to a no-budget producer. At least there are plenty of yachts. . . but can I find a *free* one? Will Technicolour Hollywood cut me a deal?

Hello, L.A., you crummy old town!

L.A. is my Bedford Falls. I'm dying to escape, but I keep getting pulled back here. The only alternatives seem to be New York (too noisy, expensive, don't know anyone there), Chicago (a theatre town—great actors—if you can catch them before they emigrate to L.A. or New York. But I don't know anyone there), London (film financing there is a Europudding nightmare). Too bad I can't speak French (I like French films, and I think they might like mine). Australia has quite a few women directors. . .? I had hoped to return to L.A. "A Star" (or even a small planet), but at least I now have a decent film to show off. I find a one-bedroom apartment in Venice, where Ray Bradbury lived when he was my age (gang wars have kept rents reasonable). My first time without roommates in two years— ah, peace! No more living with people I can't stand! Except now I have to go to Women in Film breakfasts and Independent Feature Project mixers every night and mingle with people I can't stand; I must find a new crew. Everyone I knew has left L.A., left the industry, or died. No one understands a word I say ("Where are you *from?*"). I've been away so long, I can't remember which words are American and which are Glaswegian, so I watch *Roseanne* for vocabulary lessons.

Fifty (out of fifty-two) agents ask for tapes of *Pay Your Rent, Beethoven*, but either don't watch it, return it smashed (do they, or the postmen, stomp on it?), or the usual no response. Now I lose $3 in postage and a $5 a tape with every attempt, rather than just a 29-cent letter.

But what I really want to do is *claim* I'm a producer!

Whiners in Film and IFP have offices far more glamourous than the GFVW—but neither actually makes films, has equipment, or offers grants (unless you're an *ethnic* minority. Women make up 51% of the population, so, presumably, we're in charge!). WIF doesn't even have screenings of members' films, just a gala once in a while to raise funds for any cause other than FILMMAKING—God forbid women should be *self-promoting*! No, we can only do things for the *community*. There are no women in film in Women in Film, and the Independent Feature Project has no feature projects (or even short projects).

I get lots of advice at Women in Film breakfasts: "Become a famous actress, like Penny Marshall, Barbra Streisand and Jodie Foster, and then they'll *let* you direct!" Oh, okay—SNAP! I'll do that tomorrow! I pay $10 for their donut and cinnamon roll breakfasts, and then spend the rest of the day freaked out by the sugar. I meet a fleet of potential producers for *$on for Sail* (*everyone* in Women in Film is a producer). I quickly go through nine fast-talkers who each last less than two weeks before they take a real (paying) job, or I fire them for incompetence. I eventually settle on two women who produce Women in Film breakfasts and LOVE talking on the phone (an activity I *hate*). They talk, and talk, and talk. I've already negotiated prices with vendors, but they say they can do better. They call the vendors, inform them how lucky they are to be working on their film, and the vendors do better. They raise their prices. The braggarts get bored discussing logistics, but become giddy discussing the directors' chairs they're going to sit in on the set. Still, I have to have help organizing my first 35mm shoot, with my biggest crew yet (four in the camera crew alone—Panavision, as part of its New Filmmakers program, is lending us a Gold camera, God bless 'em).

Miraculously, at a Women in Film breakfast, I meet a woman who has actually worked in films: Shirley, a D.P. As I drive to a Thai restaurant to meet her for lunch, Shirley comes storming along in her monster truck, blares her horn and curses me for daring to drive only five miles an hour over the speed limit. In the restaurant, Shirley is as ebullient as Billy Connolly, and doesn't recognize me as the Honda Driver she tried to annihilate three minutes earlier. I debate whether I should hire a D.P. with such a bad temper and poor visual memory, but she does have a good reel—no comedy, but lots of fight scenes and wildlife. Later, Shirley tells someone at a WIF breakfast that I wisely didn't write a film called *Daughter for Sail* because I'm hip and I know films about women won't sell. I've never said, or even thought, anything like that. Why is Shirley putting words in my mouth and making such stupid presumptions? She's supposed to be on *our* side!

I get the rest of the crew from my new and improved notices: "Pay," (a whopping $20 per day) "short shooting schedule, copy of film, *catered food*, chocolate-laden craft services and fun, fun, *fun!*"

Hair in the Projector

John Vickery comes on board as the $on's Dad. The $on is a great young actor named Patrick Todd, hot off the boat from Chicago (so to speak), and Irene Roseen and Gordon Jorgenson round out the cast.

I call the producers to discuss logistics for our biggest and most expensive day—filming the opening daydream scene on the yacht. I've (secretly) nicknamed one of my producers *The Chicken* (she has a phobia that's a small inconvenience for a producer in Los Angeles: she doesn't drive ["I almost crashed once!" (like, who in L.A. hasn't?)]). The Chicken waits until now to inform me of another phobia: she never gets within three miles of the Pacific Ocean ("I almost drowned once!" [like, who hasn't?]), so she can't *possibly* have anything to do with the boat scenes and, please, don't even *mention* water, or she'll have nightmares! (God, my suspicions were correct—she *didn't* read the script. . . or even the script's title! Well, no, she's been telling the title to vendors. . . I guess this dyslexic shopaholic thought she was working on *Sun for Sale*.) Then, the other producer informs me *she* can't work on Yacht Day—she can't *possibly* miss her Women in Film breakfast! Then The Chicken says she can't attend *any* production meetings until shooting begins (when it will be a little late for meetings): "I can't go out in public until I get my cornrows done!" When I suggest, *perhaps it wasn't such a good idea to undergo an eight-hour hair operation the day before we shoot?* she screams at me, "*You don't tell me what to do with my hair!*"

I tell the "producers" not to worry about their hair or breakfasts or the color of their directors chairs—they are off the film. They promptly get on their phones and tell Fotokem, Agfa, and the sound transfer facility that *$on for Sail* has been canceled, and warn them, if that Jürgen calls, don't do business with her, she's a *liar* and a *crook!* The sales reps reply, well, she gave us a $4,000 deposit two weeks ago. . . *and you are. . .?* I never thought *my* money, my pathetic little pocket change, would sway anyone (I guess in Hollywood, even a little money talks). Instead of focusing on minute details like rehearsing my actors, I have to spend the day before Day One phoning the vendors and apologizing for hiring such nutcases. They reassure me, "Never mind; it was kind of amusing, how much they hate you!" as though they're *impressed* I could inspire such venom. The vendors even lower their prices back down to the poor groveling independent filmmaker rates I initially negotiated!

Hello, Dolly!

At the end of Day One, Patrick Todd's slimeball agent telephones. I'm paying the actors "scale plus ten" (meaning SAG minimum wage, plus an extra 10% to their agents). Patrick's greedy little shit agent claims we agreed to pay Patrick the SAG $485 daily minimum *each day*, for all five days, not SAG's *weekly* rate of $1,685. I try to reason with the scumbag; why would an independent short filmmaker do *that*? He says he's calling Patrick and pulling him off the film. I broke Rule Number One: never let an actor set foot on the set without a contract! Do I ask Patrick (who I know will agree to work for the weekly rate, as we had agreed) to tell his agent to go fuck himself, and make Patrick even more tense the day before his big scene? No, I decide to pay up, and not risk freaking out my leading man. I try to shrug off losing a month's housecleaning wages. I *try*.

Filming goes as well as a no-budget shoot can. As usual, there's no spare cash, which produces several near heart attacks, and I, the director-producer, have a few split-personality arguments with myself (*I need another take*—"*No*, we're falling behind schedule!"). We have one 18-hour day when Shirley replaces our planned pans and tilts with elaborate dolly shots, which I did not authorize (I knew we wouldn't have enough time), and *then* she insists on a 10-hour turn-around—which means we get to Mother's Beach the next day four hours later than planned to shoot the climactic scene, and the lighting *sucks* and we only have time to get two dull master shots. Production is my least favorite part of filmmaking (although journalists only like taking pictures of you at this stage. Staring at a Steenbeck, sitting by the phone waiting for the negative cutter to confirm, yes, they have indeed accidentally destroyed your best shot and you have to re-edit. . . those moments don't make the best photos.). Production is where a director's dreams die. Just beat the clock. Just get the shot. Your actors ask an intelligent question and the sun is disappearing and you have to say, "Just do it the way we planned it!" and all that Old Vic training goes right out the window. But when the actors bring the characters to life, when someone on the crew comes up with a great idea, it makes all the pain worthwhile.

The two-hour charter on the yacht costs as much as one month's rent on my apartment, but I almost have fun. Best of all is going to dailies. . . yes, dailies—*daily* dailies! I've been very indulgent on this film: no film from a fridge, a caterer (it's their first job), one-day-old bagels—*nothing but second-best for* my *crew!* After one look at the 35mm footage, I am *never* going back to lowly 16mm! And certainly not *video*. Wow, it looks just like a real movie! Shirley has been slow, bitchy, and added unnecessary shots (when they processed all that wasted footage, I could almost hear Fotokem's cash register go *ca-ching! Ca-CHING!!*). But she sure can light. She did one especially nice dolly (she spent 90 minutes setting it up). Of course, I'm going to cut 80% off the head of that shot; a pretty picture, but it adds nothing to the story.

Chop Chop!

This is the first time I've had a full editing crew. The assistant editor says, "It's nice to be working on something that's not a total piece of junk!" Wow, if I keep improving, someday, someone on my crew will actually say, "This film is *good*!"

Instead of writing a new screenplay, I spend Christmas organizing my production receipts and filling out film festival entry forms. God, these endless piles of paperwork will kill me. I wish I had a business-minded brother like Roy Disney, Sydney Chaplin or Theo Van Gogh. I'm going to be hocking *$on for Sail* full-time for at least a year. Unless I can jump way up in budget, I can't work with SAG actors again. Although they only ate one-tenth of the budget (thank God I only had four actors), that was $6,000 I desperately needed for film festival entry fees, printing posters and photos, video copies, postage, plane tickets to film festivals, rental cars, motels, meals out, taking time off maid work to work on publicity. . . Still, barring any major act of God, we should come in way under budget, and I can take three months off cleaning toilets to get Discovered.

CHAPTER 20

1994, Age 27

Cannes of Worms

John Vickery and Patrick Todd in *$on for Sail*

Jürgen vs. Mickey Mouse

Our terrific composer/sound designer finishes his work on *$on for Sail* (yeah, he's a guy... well, nobody's perfect!). After only two semi-begging phone calls, we've secured a free mix from Todd-A.O./Glenn Glenn! 24-track Dolby Stereo, here I come!

The day before we mix, God acts, in the form of a nice big earth-quake. All of Todd A.O.'s sound stages are out of commission; Free Mix Nixed. Todd A.O. tells me, "Maybe in six months... or nine..."

With so many stages in L.A. crippled, there are no free or cheap mixes anywhere on the planet. *Pay Your Rent Beethoven's* prolonged post-production nearly killed me. I keep phoning around and risk being irritating. Finally, one company's bad mood saves me: Cinesound, a small but excellent company, has been bullied and yelled at by Disney for months, and they've been looking for some way to stick it to the Mouse. With one day's notice, they bump Mickey, and in goes *$on for Sail!* They charge me $300 an hour (probably half of what Disney was paying, but thirty times what I'm paid per hour as a maid). Our mixer, Mark Rozett, is only paid for eight hours, but he likes our film ("Hey, this film is *good!*") and gives us three free hours.

$on for Sail comes out okay. . . but just okay. It's a good film, but I don't love it. The script seems kinda forced (which it was). Again, like in 1989, I was just dying to make a *film*—not necessarily *$on for Sail.* I have a cast and crew screening at Fotokem. Of course, the thing everyone loves the most about the film is the character of the $on. That's without a single word changed in the script. Despite Patrick Todd's sleezeball agent and the Northridge Earthquake, I've come in $123 below budget! Now, it's time to make money for the publicity, get Discovered, and get a feature made. I beg Patrick, "Get a commercial, or soap—*anything*—to help publicize the film!" He looks agog—he was expecting *me* to help *him*, for the film to be a hit, for me to become a star director to help *him* get a decent agent!

The Butler Did It

I'm promoted to Butler, covering for an elderly butler who's undergoing radiation treatments three days a week. I get an extra $2 an hour and directing practice (directing the other servants). Every time I show The Rich and Mighty in, I'm greeted with, "I've never seen a *woman* butler before!"

I strut into Women in Film breakfasts "fresh off my latest film." Women were the writer, director and producer (that would be me), editor, D.P., 2nd A.C., production manager, 1st A.D., art director, costume designer, make-up artist. . . do I get the applause and *oooh*ing and *aaaahhh*ing a woman director deserves for such a feat? Nope!—I get, "Why did you make $ON *for Sail*?" and "Why did you make a *short* film?" I reply, "Because I bloody well felt like it, and with the money I had, I could either make a great-looking short, or a crappy-looking feature!" The vacant looks. A woman wearing Armani sniffs, "When I hear someone has made so *many* shorts, I wonder, *why hasn't she gotten a feature*? It implies you don't know what you're doing!" I bite my tongue, play the optimist and chant, "Art, man, I had to make some *art*!" (I should have said, "Go fuck yourself, *bitch*!") The WIF programming committee refuses to screen our film. I point out that the second lead is a woman —*and* over 50 (*shock! Horror!*), but no dice.

Soda Jerks

Women in Committees (er, uh, Film) sanctions a woman who holds directing workshops in her house. . . only $5 to cover the cost of chips and soda (should directors be eating this crap?). There, I meet a woman the same age as me who has directed a feature! She looks away and mumbles, "It was just *Slumber Party Massacre 3*." Well, that's *some*thing! *I'm* impressed! *I* couldn't even get a rejection letter from Roger Corman! But. . . is it not worth it if you can't jump up and down with pride and wave a video of your film and yell, "Hey, everybody, *look at what I made!*". . . ? Nah, in this town, it's better to have a feature, *any* feature, to distinguish yourself from the wannabe masses. Forty-five minutes into the "workshop," there's been zero talk of directing. The women rattle on and on about personal problems, until I finally ask, "Excuse me, have I accidentally come to 'Women in *Therapy*'?" An hour later, they're *still* bitching, so I go home to watch a movie.

I hire a film festival consultant named Bob Hawk, who hawks himself as the man who discovered Kevin Smith and *Clerks*. I figure he'll justify his fee by recommending festivals that will (or won't) like *$on for Sail*. His great pearls of wisdom? "Enter festivals that have no entry fees and offer cash prizes." No, *duh*!

I get a parcel from London: a copy of the new book *World Cinema: Diary of a Day*. The British Film Institute asked people in the film industry to write a diary on June 10, 1993. They published my entry in the book! No payment (of course), just one free copy of the book and something new to put on my resume. My entry has one big distinction: I'm by far the least successful person in the book! In fact, I'd better get *Curl Up and Dye* made soon, or they'll edit me out of future printings. I can now claim to be a published author—and only 31 pages away from Terry "Dad" Gilliam!

Finally, I have a film that qualifies for Academy Award Consideration (Super-8 is not worthy of Oscar, but 35mm *f* is). All I have to do is pay the Laemmle Theatres $100 to show my film for three nights—*after* the last feature of the night, when people are falling asleep. I beg the Laemmles to show it *before* the feature, when some Academy member might actually see my film ("Remember all the great popcorn scooping I did for you in 1987?"), but no will do. This requirement by the Academy is just a meaningless hoop to jump through, and it's risky; more often than not, the films get scratched (the projectionist, annoyed by having to stay late, is not exactly careful with the prints). The popcorn the casts and crews buy must make it profitable for the theatre. No wonder so many young filmmakers go bankrupt in their quest. Like a young ice skater, you have to take such huge financial gambles. Yes, you can rub shoulders and network with bigwigs at benefits—*if* you can afford the $500 plate, and the clothes to get in the door. Where do you draw the line and say those words forbidden in Hollywood (which send thee directly to the bottom of the sludge pile): "*I can't afford it!*"?

No Cannes Do

The IFP announces a program called "Independents at Cannes" (is that an oxymoron?). $710 gets you a market pass and one screening of your film. I ask the IFP organizers, "Do people *buy* shorts at the market?" "Oh, *all* the time!" they assure me. So I bring both *$on for Sail* and *Pay Your Rent, Beethoven* to Cannes. My films are scheduled to screen mid-way through the market. From Day One of the Market, it rains non-stop, forcing people to seek shelter and actually watch movies. One hour before my *$on for Sail* screening, the sun suddenly comes out, and everyone runs to the beach. The only people who come to my film are two transvestites (the stars of the film screening immediately after mine*)*. The three film buyers who come to see *Pay Your Rent, Beethoven* walk out muttering, "I sot it vas a sequel to ze dog movie!"

I decide to try the IFP Market in September. I fork over $400 for one *$on for Sail* screening at the Anjelika, and another $400 for a quarter-page ad in the market brochure. Despite submitting my film months before the deadline, I'm given a 9am Sunday screening in the town that never sleeps—except at on Sundays at 9am. And there are no refunds, *ha ha ha!* Tough!—*take what we give you and thank us!* So I pay another $400 for an additional screening at the Tribeca Film Center. They give me a 4pm Friday slot—anyone wanting to come will have to swim against Friday afternoon traffic. Five people come to the Tribeca screening. Chatting to them afterwards, I learn they are all Tribeca staff. Even though none of them particularly liked it, I think paying each person $80 to watch my short film seems a bit excessive. At my Rise 'n Shine 9am Sunday screening, three brave hung-over souls stumble in (all filmmakers: their way of thanking me for being the only person to come to *their* screenings). I must say, I am impressed by the IFP's efficiency at ripping off its members. We were wooed with the promise of meeting acquisitions folks, but acquisitioners remove their identifying badges so they won't be bothered by pesky filmmakers. I drop by the IFP office and ask if they're going to use all the money they've made here and at Cannes to create a production grant. More vacant looks.

Going to markets with short films was *dumb*. Miramax is looking for features they can make lots of money off. One *hears* about filmmakers getting a feature after making a promising short. . . uh, but not me, or anyone I've ever met. I can't get the D-Girls to even watch a video. For my first feature, I'm going to have my own screening at 7:30pm, on a studio lot, with food—no, with *booze!*

I hire an industry consultant to help me figure out how to manage my career; but this woman can't even manage her own daughter, a creature who bursts in every five minutes whining about not being allowed to go out with her friends, until finally the consultant caves in and lets her go (*hey. . .* maybe her daughter is simply demonstrating how *I* need to act in order to get ahead in Hollywood! Francis Ford Coppola probably just kept storming through Paramount's gate until they finally said, *Here, take $3 million, just* go away!). The consultant says she really has only one piece of advice for me: "Join a *wonderful* organization called Women in Film!"

Hannibal Lector's Manager Bites My Ear Off

There *is* one organization I want to join: BAFTA, the British Academy of Film and Television Arts. According to *The Hollywood Reporter*, they have tea parties with cucumber sandwiches, and free screenings. It would be a good way to meet people who can form complete sentences (that's a lot to ask for in this town). You need two signatures on your application from BAFTA members who will vouch that you won't sing the lyrics to *My County 'tis of Thee* when the band plays *God Save the Queen*. The only person I know for sure is a member is Anthony Hopkins. My piano teacher said Hopkins came to her Presbyterian church last year for a fundraiser (See? - the Presbyterians *have* gone Hollywood!) and he was very nice, and I can drop Jonathan Miller's name (Hopkins starred in Jonathan's *Othello*). I write a humble letter about my qualifications, include a video of my short films, and send my application (with SASEs) in care of Hopkins's manager. Two days later, the Manager phones me and shouts so loudly, I have to hold the receiver three feet away from my head. "What gives you the *nerve* to write to Mr. Hopkins? *Who do you think you are? Mr. Hopkins doesn't know you, he does not sign applications for* amateur *film makers!"* (Sherlock Holmes was an amateur. . . he also wasn't real, but that's beside the point.) Wow! I've read about Hollywood temper tantrums, but this is the first time I've ever be on the receiving end. *I must be doing something right!* You're in Hollywood now! To preserve my hearing, I lay the receiver down on my desk, go to the kitchen, and wash a week's worth of dishes. When I come back to the phone, the Manager has just started to warm up. After a brief pause, I cheerfully say, "I'm sorry, I didn't quite catch that—would you mind repeating it?" He splutters a few how-dare-yous, and I hang up in case a film festival director is trying to get through.

CHAPTER 21

1995, Age 28

Oscar Hates Me

Film Festival Short Circuits

$on for Sail is accepted into the Palm Springs Film Festival. Except for my composer/sound designer, none of the cast or crew can (or, *will*) come to hand out flyers and help pack the house. Press, man, I need press, I need publicity! I can't afford to make *$on for Sail* buttons, baseball caps, t-shirts and four-color posters; but talk is cheap, so I sneak into the festival's press room and call all the television stations. Two local news stations send out crews to interview me.

My first screening at the festival goes well; the audience is mostly senior citizens. So that's why I got into this festival: *$on for Sail* appeals more to older people, who laugh out loud at the $on's predicament; younger people think it's a horror story, their worst fear come true: Dad demands reparation payments for a lifetime of ingratitude. As I pack up my car after the screening, two old women who have seen me on last night's news ask, "Why are you leaving, when your film is screening again tomorrow?" I tell them I have no money, and the festival only puts short film makers up for one night at the Motel 6 (although they've given me the usual fancy shopping bag full of soaps, shampoos and cosmetics [why cosmetics, when the vast majority of directors are men? Because goodie bags are actually offerings to the neglected wife/girlfriend/daughter of the Director]. Why is there never *food*, movie tickets and rent money in the film makers' goodie bags?! Because, rather than hosing us down in a car wash so the little unwashed artists won't contaminate their ballrooms, they've thoughtfully provided us with the *tools* to civilize ourselves. *Give a man a fish, he'll eat for a day. Teach a man to fish. . .* [he'll sit in a boat drinking beer all day]). The women proclaim, "That's not right!" (they mean the one-night-only motel situation, not the injustice of the goodie bags). After one quick phone call by these blue-haired angels, I am installed in a five-star bungalow with a jacuzzi in the bathroom that normally goes for $1,300 a night (twice my monthly rent).

I think my film is by far the best short of the festival, but I can forget about winning *an award*, or getting a good review. These days, festival judges and critics automatically view anything in focus with suspicion. Independent films must be gloomy, with endings so downbeat that unless you want to slit your throat in the ladies room afterwards, they smack of crass commercialism and pandering to "the lowest common denominator." People like to boast, "We love it because *we're* brilliant and *we* get the auteur's *intentions*" (never mind that the actual result is a pretentious bore). It has also become a point of pride to see just how bad you can make your film's production values (the *Clerks* phenomenon). Grainy images mean you're *artistic*, not too lazy to learn how to use a light meter. Focus? *Overrated.* Perfect continuity and a three-act structure? *You've obviously gone Hollywood.* Good naturalistic acting? *Bor-ing!* A tripod? *Sell out!* A *real* artist at a party informs me, "Making a film like yours is *easy*— it's the *true* artist who can dispense with all that 'technique!'" Dummy me, I thought making a film look and sound good was simply being competent. Young filmmakers these days never admit they made a mistake (*Whooooaaa, I really fucked up that shot, didn't I?*), but adopt the quotable, printable motto, "I *designed* it like that!" It was their *intention*, not laziness, bad planning, or lack of funds.

Even though both *$on for Sail* and *Pay Your Rent, Beethoven* were rejected by the Sundance Film Festival, I've been told, *You can't miss its networking opportunities!* Go to a film festival without a film? That sounds like self-flagellation! But I go. Yesterday, a private bungalow with a king-sized bed: tonight, a sleeping bag on the Women in Film condo floor. How the mighty have fallen. I can't afford a festival pass (all the films will be at the Laemmle or multiplex in a few months, anyway), so I work as a volunteer, like Steven Soderbergh did (although, when *he* volunteered, he had *sex, lies and videotape* in the festival, the film that started all this "independent film" madness—pretty good for a guy who didn't even know how to use the "Shift" key). Sundance is a madhouse, and buyers have come to buy, not talk to a "wannabe." In the filmmaker's lounge, I spot John Sayles giving an interview about his new film, *The Secret of Roan Inish*. I've been taught to never interrupt people. . . but Mom, this is *John Sayles*! So I say "excuse me" to the journalist and thank Sayles for *Matewan*. Wow, I met a Real-Live *great* filmmaker!

Not Ralph Nader . . . but close

At the parties, I'm asked by everyone, "Where did you go to film school?" I reply, "Wroughten Films—I made 28 shorts!" (I imagine film students' reply. . . *I went to the AFI, but I don't know how to block a scene—I was too busy taking meetings at CAA.*) I was never asked that before *The New York Times* started writing articles about film schools. Scam artists have discovered there are big bucks to be taken from rich wannabe filmmakers, or even lower-class ones who can take out huge student loans. The newspapers neglect to mention how the students will spend the rest of their lives paying back the interest on these loans.

Home, and I collapse in my rocking chair for three weeks with pneumonia. Notwithstanding the bungalow and jacuzzi, trying to do two film festivals back to back with no money was a bad idea. I wonder about my future in L.A. (or if I even have one). Maybe my career is progressing: I *am* getting nicer and nicer rejection letters (and always written on *their* stationary). People don't come to L.A. to make great films; they come to make great wads of cash and become famous and party and stoke their egomaniacal bonfires. At Sundance, I heard no talk about the quality of the films, just the quality of the deals and what film sold for the most. I'm sick to death of working as a domestic so I can afford to work in show business. My next venture will be commercial. . . good quality commerciality, but no more shorts, *ever*!

No Oscar for Thee

The day after the Oscars, I realize the Academy hasn't returned my $1,000 *$on for Sail* print. I drive over to Oscar H.Q., where the dopey guy in charge of storage pokes around for five seconds and says he must have returned it. I demand he look for at least one full minute. He manages to uncover an old comic book he misplaced. As I leave, I brush against the door, and a film can crashes on the floor. *My baby!* The metal carrier has a huge dent in it. The dude says, "Oh, I was using your film as a doorstop! Now I'm gonna hafta find something else to hold the door open. . . " I'm so angry, I can't even muster the energy to yell at him. When I ask if he's joking, he says, "No, I've been tripping over your print for the last two weeks!" and he *kicks* my print. The only way I refrain from choking this asshole is by focusing on getting my film the hell out of there. I can't believe the Academy hired such a bozo—I'd expect something like this from Cannes (the projectionist there stole my metal reel and carrier, and returned my film in a plastic garbage bag; Fotokem said I was lucky to get my film back at all).

I check out my print at Fotokem. It's so dirty, the projectionist says it looks like been screening in a shopping mall multiplex for six months. When the Academy president, Arthur Hiller, spoke of the importance of film preservation at the Oscars, he obviously wasn't referring to films that failed to get Oscar nominations. I write to Hiller, asking the Academy to pay for cleaning my print, and enclose the $50 bill. Two weeks later, I get a long letter from Hiller, insisting the Academy *never* treats prints badly. . . but he also encloses a check for $50! I'm glad I won't have to picket the AMPAS library (the best film school in town).

Miramax, Feed Your Children!

I journey to Saturn (Pasadena) to Vrooman's Books for a signing of the groovy memoir *Lost in Place* by Mark Salzman (a fellow cellist, martial artist and eccentric). There, I meet Kayo Hatta, the director of *Picture Bride*, a low-budget but beautifully-shot film (oh Kayo, *you fool!*). Kayo later runs up to guy handing out passes for a free movie preview screening. When the guy asks Kayo, "Do you work in the film industry?" she answers a firm, "No, I'm an accountant!" Despite having a film distributed by Miramax, Kayo hasn't a dime, and the $7 saved will buy her some much-needed food. My God, is *this* what I have to look forward to? I always tell the free screening folks I'm a particle physicist. My D.P. Shirley always smiles and tells them, "No, I can't go—*I'm in the industry!*" which makes me wonder about her ego and her refusal to suppress it for the sake of a free movie. Kayo and I go over to Virgin Records and rearrange the CD racks to give more prominence to *Picture Bride*'s soundtrack: surely, Madonna has plenty of food money and wouldn't mind yielding two of her twelve CD rack displays to help a starving artist?

Pay Your Rent, Vsych

I decide to take yet another whack at the *Pay Your Rent, Beethoven* feature script—and three weeks later, it's done! What a relief. I was worried that fifteen years of research was going to result in a hopelessly convoluted mess, but no, it produced my best screenplay! I did everything I set out to do—write a historically accurate serious comedy with room for lots of little-known Beethoven hits (they'll make a great soundtrack), and make it not too expensive to produce: it's not set in one room in Fresno, but it does have a lot of scenes in the country, no car chases, hardly any horses (thank God Beethoven couldn't ride one), no camels, and only one big concert (I see lots of out-of-focus, incorrectly-attired extras and cardboard people). The only bummer is, apart from the title and some trouble with his landlords, it has nothing in common with my short film—meaning I can't use the short film to show what the feature would be like: financiers would expect a slapstick comedy.

I spend a month throwing my *PYR,B* screenplay to the wolves. Well, *that* was another colossal waste of time. No one wants to even read it. It has three strikes against it: 1) Hollywood hears *Beethoven* and thinks "St. Bernard" (damn that movie!). 2) *Amadeus* still casts a long shadow. Hollywood feels the American moviegoing public can only handel (ha ha ha) one movie about a classical composer every twenty-five years. 3) *Immortal Beloved* (Gary Oldman was good, but must have been on drugs when he read the script). Producers have the perfect excuse: "Oh yeah, there was a film about Beethoven—it bombed—*next*!" God, why must I have such sucky timing?

Pay Your Rent, Beethoven (the short) is my biggest hit internationally, and gets into lots of foreign festivals (I can't go myself—no free plane tickets for *short* filmmakers), but in my own country, *wipeout*. Still, I decide to help Laemmle renovate their bathrooms, and pay for an Oscar-qualifying screening. They pair it with the brilliant *Persuasion*, which takes place, coincidentally, in the same year as *PYR,B*. I know the chances of an Oscar nomination without any "names" involved in my film is zero (celebrities have started making shorts, realizing it's a quick way to get on that red carpet and promote themselves as "Academy Award Winner. . . "). Still, this is the first time I've seen *PYR,B* in a theatre in two years; $100 is chicken feed to remind myself that I really *am* a filmmaker.

"Pastorical-comical, historical-pastoral, tragical-historical, tragical-comical-historical pastoral. . . "

The IFP has a "Pitching to the Pros" seminar: you pay $150 and pitch your film ideas to two companies (randomly selected by the IFP, *natürlich*—and no refunds). As I walk down the corridor to my first session, I pass two 23-year-old guys talking. The guy with thinning hair says to his heavily-gelled friend, "I like your hair! How d'ya get it like that?" His friend says, "Man, I have to sleep on my right side all night. I shove pillows against my back so I won't roll over, and I set my alarm so I can wake up every hour and comb it back into shape!"

I pitch *Curl Up and Dye* to the Samuel Goldwyn Company. The two 23-year-old D-Girls say, "Well, *we* like the idea, but no *guy* is going to want to see that film—they're not interested in hair!"

I reply, "What, are you *crazy*?! They're *way* more concerned about their hair than women: they've got to worry about going bald! Here—wait a minute. . . !" and I run out to lasso the two guys to testify, but they've disappeared.

Next, I pitch to another company that shall remain nameless (ADDIS-WECHSLER). The D-Boy says not to bother pitching him anything that stars anyone over forty (which *Curl Up and Dye*, unfortunately, does), and no "mixed genres" (i.e. comical-tragical-historical *Pay Your Rent, Beethoven*), so I pitch *Arch*. "It's about a girl who—"

The D-Boy says, "Oh, we already have one of those."

I say, "One of what?"

"One of those films, you know, with a girl. You got anything else?"

Now I am 29. The number of years I've lived has now surpassed the number of films I've made. I thought if my film tally stayed ahead of my age, I would never die. I feel the Reaper breathing down my neck. . .

CHAPTER 22

1996, Age 29

Bat Out of Hell

Showdown at Denny's

At the IFP New Year's party, I ask Dawn Hudson, the party queen of the IFP. . . sorry, I mean *President*. . . please, will her organization (IFP members don't get to elect the President or the board members, so I daren't say *our organization*) turn the music down thirty decibels so the filmmakers' hearing won't be permanently damaged, and create a feature film funding scheme à la the Glasgow Film and Video Workshop (then we would *really* be a feature project, not just a bunch of party animals)? Hudson lifts her nose, walks to the D.J., and orders him to turn the volume *up*.

At a quieter party, I meet a real producer (he has an office and posters from real films crediting him as an associate producer). He doesn't like my writing, but likes my directing (it's always one or the other, never both [or, more likely, they just don't want a woman having so much fun]). He needs a director for a feature he's written. At last, my first offer! Unfortunately, his screenplay, about a student filmmaker shooting a porn movie, makes me physically ill. Shirley and my composer/sound designer want me to do it so they'll have paying jobs with a non-psychotic director. The problem is, I may become psychotic if I have to read another page of this script, let alone direct it. I guess this guy wants me because I'm cheap, I always finish on schedule, and he thinks having a woman direct this sexist shit will somehow make it okay. I'm not crazy about the writer being my boss (if he were Alan Bennett, that'd be another matter). I agree to meet him at Denny's Restaurant (well, gotta start somewhere). The writer-producer is rude to waitress for absolutely no reason (just think how he'll treat my crew) and physically attacks a toy-dispensing machine when it fails to give him exactly the toy he wants (just think how he'll treat *me*). So I pass at what might be my one chance to direct a feature, but at least my stomach pains vanish.

I thought if I worked hard and mastered my craft, eventually, I would be Discovered. But I have no awards to waive around (The Princes Trust is not recognized by the D-Girls: "*You mean Diana's ex-husband? His* truss?"). A short is never going to get reviewed by the trades or the *Los Angeles Times*. I've tried all the right steps. The only thing I haven't tried is starting at the bottom as a production assistant. It would mean months of working for free, and being forever ridiculed as a plucky little secretary who tried on bigger boots. *And hey, she's so good at her job, let's keep her at it!* You would think all those years of dealing with Dad would make me really good at handling Hollywood idiots, but it's simply worn down my skin and made me less tolerant of prima donnery. I feel like I'm dying here. Any excitement I once had for films is fading fast. "Independent" films are starting to resemble the Studios' films (i.e. *stupid*—not good-looking). Constantly, I think, "I can't wait to have some success so I can get the hell out of Hell!" And I'm tired of sleeping on my hallway floor to avoid bullets. L.A. has progressed from a place where you don't want to carry too much money in your wallet, to making sure you carry at least $50 so *when* you're robbed, they won't kill you. I dream of moving somewhere pretty, like Seattle.

As though they've heard me, *Newsweek's* new cover story is about Seattle being one of the best places to live in America. They have lots of bookstores and arthouse movie theatres, and less crime. Seattle is the most literate place in the USA, and it has fir trees, lakes, and rain (good writing weather). *Bill Nye the Science Guy* tapes there, and *Northern Exposure* used to film there, so there must be idle crew members and some film equipment lying about. It's the same time zone as L.A. and there are cheap flights there on Alaska Airlines (I even have an Alaska Airlines credit card—*it's a sign!*). I pack my films and scripts into my Honda and drive North.

The Bills

I find a $690-a-month apartment with a million-dollar view of Lake Washington and the Cascade Mountains. Heaven!—but, as I sign my lease, my landlord chirps, "The *Seattle Times* said that the weekend box office was good!" (Is there *no* escape?!)

To pay the moving company, I go downtown to sell my coin and stamp collections. As I kick myself for not dressing better or putting on lipstick to get more money from the buyer, two men enter the elevator. My sweatpants render me invisible, and the men talk about how *Bill* is buying stocks in a new internet company. Having quickly immersed myself in Seattle culture, I know that the *Bill* on everyone's lips here is, alas, not *Nye*, but *Gates*. I take the money from my coin and stamp sale, stop by my bank, and withdraw all my money. I run to a stockbroker and buy Bill's stock. Four days later, I sell it for $18,719. I want to go condo-shopping immediately, but. . . maybe I should make a feature? Can I make *Arch*? I'm worried that a low-concept drama will get lost in the sea of "independent" films.

Almost Dead!

Seattle has their own version of *Saturday Night Live* called *Almost Live!* I write thirty-five sketches and drop them off at the station so they can reject them at their leisure. Maybe I could expand my sketch about female Superheroines (Mother Nature, The Librarian and The Chocolatier) and Supervillianesses (Virginia Svelte, Cosmetic Chick and The Doucher) into a series! Nah, t.v. wouldn't allow such rampant feminism.

While I'm in writing-mode, might as well pen a few sketches on spec and get rejected by *Bill Nye the Science Guy*, too!. . .

Smell Episode: Movie Trailer

ANNOUNCER
Coming soon from U-Nyeversal Pictures—*On the Nose.*

INT. BACK SEAT OF CAR. A man with a busted nose laments his fate to his brother.

BROTHER
The fight was close—you lost by a nose.

BRANDO
You're talking through your nose!

BROTHER
Bill, I know your nose is out of joint, but don't thumb your nose at boxing. Just keep your nose to the grindstone and—

BRANDO
Why'd ya make me take a nosedive?

BROTHER
Don't stick your nose where it don't belong—

BRANDO
You don't understand—I was up to snuff! I could have smelled the roses! I could have been a perfumer! Who nose what I could have accomplished?!

BROTHER
Bill, wake up and smell the coffee!

ANNOUNCER
On the Nose—nosing into theatres this summer!

The Sounds of Science

INT. LABORATORY. Bill Nye, in his tux, dazzles the audience with a few dance steps.

> ANNOUNCER
> From Not That Bad Records, Bill Nye croons.
> THE SOUNDS OF SCIENCE—scientifically
> valid vocalizations of illogical, unscientific
> emotions. Bill Nye, the Minstrel of Science
> warbles, as only he can, ballads of brain over
> brawn!

Bill, dressed in cap and gown. Four women wearing nerdy glasses throw themselves at his feet.

> BILL
> "You Gotta Be Valedictorian [a Football
> Hero], if you want the intelligent [beautiful]
> girls!"

> ANNOUNCER
> Outpourings of environmental responsibleness!

Bill on his bicycle:

> BILL
> "Baby, You Can Ride [Drive] My Bike [Car]!"
> (he rings the bike's bell)

> ANNOUNCER
> Strains. . . and we mean, *strains*. . . of genuine
> affection—

Bill wraps a tape measure around a woman's head as though measuring her brain.

> BILL
> "I Love Yoooooooouuuuuu For Scientific [Sen-
> timental] Reasons."

The Woman Director

ANNOUNCER
Arias of unparalleled loving generosity.

Bill is hooked up to a blood bag.

BILL
"I can't give you anything but blood [love],
baby!"

ANNOUNCER
Melodies of physiological correctness—

Bill holds a stethoscope over his chest.

BILL
"Lub—dub! [Zing!] went the muscles [strings]
of my heart!"

ANNOUNCER
—*and* political correctness!

M.S. Bill plays the piano, a woman's legs draped over the piano.

BILL
"That's why the lady—"

Pull back to reveal the woman is dressed in lab coat and safety glasses.

BILL
"—is a biologist [tramp]!"

ANNOUNCER
And sorrowful songs of unrequited yearnings.

Bill holds a newspaper with headline: "NOBEL PRIZES ANNOUNCED."

BILL
"They're giving Nobel Prizes [writing songs of
love], but not to [for] me!"

He drops the paper and covers his face, sobbing. . .

I ask a librarian if there's a Seattle equivalent of the Glasgow Film & Video Workshop. She gives me the address of 911 Media Arts. They have only video equipment, but I force myself to go to a mixer. Everyone I meet there is an experimental filmmaker ("I just want to *express* myself"), and no one thinks *Withnail & I* is funny (asking people if they like that film is my new time-saving device, along with *Do you like Buster Keaton? No? Oh, well, nice meeting you. . . [run away, run away!]*).

For women, turning the Big 3-0 is the equivalent of men turning 40, 50 and 70. I throw myself a 30th Birthday Bash at 911 Media Arts: "FREE Screening followed by reception with the Dessert Fox!" Ten people off the street wander in, and I show them *$fS* and *PYR,B*, projected on video. I introduce Shirley (visiting from L.A.) to a brand-new friend of mine (she likes *Withnail!*). They discover they both like the same kind of beer, and ditch the boring teetotaler to go bar-hopping, leaving The Chocolate Fox alone with no presents and a eight-foot-long table of uneaten desserts.

Christmas: I write feature screenplay #7, *The Root of All Evil*, about a man who goes on a murderous rampage after the government steals his entire life savings. Fueled by disgust and rage, the script only takes twelve days to write—a new record! Alas, it's not the no-budget feature I was hoping for: it needs a huge cast of great, great actors, and it's a black, black comedy—oh, *and* set in Medieval times. Hey, why don't I just throw in some camels while I'm at it! I'm not going to even bother sending it out. Save the trees.

CHAPTER 23

1997, Age 3-0

The Devil Made Me Not Do It

My goal this year is to watch a thousand films. Cable stations *Turner Classic Movies* and *American Movie Classics* and library videos make this financially possible. It's hard to blink my eyes in unison at the end of the day.

Between films, I look out my window and envision worst-case scenarios. I've acquired a devil on my shoulder that used to whisper but now barks day and night, "You'll never accomplish anything, 'cos you're a woman! Your 'brilliant career' is going to last six months, and then you'll be a laughing stock—you'll say something in an interview, it'll be misquoted and that'll be *it*! No woman director has had a life-long career, and you ain't gonna be the first! Some man will take the credit. You'll get accused of being a slut, a castrator, *and* a crybaby. Everyone will say the producer, the D.P. and the editor saved your incompetent butt. . . !"

I send my *Pay Your Rent, Beethoven* feature screenplay to Jonathan Miller ("See how *brilliant* I am!"), and ask him if he'll introduce me to people if I come to London. He sends me a postcard a few months later: "I don't *know* anyone now. I've been an exile for ten years or more. I've *not* read your script and probably never will—I don't read *anything* except books on the brain." Great, now he thinks I'm so dumb, I wouldn't even understand the word *neurology*.

Seattle's PBS station asks to show *$on for Sail* on their *Midnight Theatre*, and they pay me a staggering $200. Two small newspapers print articles about me. The *Magnolia News* article destroys my credibility amongst the 911 Media Arts crowd (it's bad enough that I've sunk to *selling* my work to *television* and *promoting* myself): the young reporter didn't know what Super-8 was, so I told her it was a low-end camera, like a camcorder. The reporter wrote that Omama gave my family a camcorder. My peers at 911 sneer, "You *lied*: camcorders weren't even invented back then!" and word quickly spreads that I am a typical Hollywood fraud. I ask the *Magnolia News* to print a correction, but they don't consider it a serious mistake. The devil on my shoulder hoots and sneers, *There's your first misquote—TOLD YA SO!*

PBS airs *$on for Sail* opposite the season début of *Saturday Night Live.*

Blame Canada

An item appears in the *Hollywood Reporter* that actually pertains to me: SAG has finally created contracts for ultra-low budget filmmakers—the actors' salaries are deferred until you make a sale (*then*, they kill you). Now there's no excuse not to make a feature. . . except for lack of a no-budget script.

In the film industry, everything and everyone in Seattle is over-priced, thanks to *Northern Exposure* and the attitude of the film commission office—"My, aren't *you* lucky we're going to *let* you shoot in our city—we did *Sleepless in Seattle*, after all!" All film production is going to Vancouver, Canada, where the government doesn't tax you to death and you get 30% more bang for your American buck. *Fraiser* has not left the building; he was too smart to ever film here! I should have headed farther North. There are good actors in Seattle, but they migrate constantly. It'd be a real crap-shoot—the actors appropriate for one of my films might not be in town when I need them.

Titanic opens. Young girls go mad for it, and the press calls Rose "a role-model" (because a boy rescues her at the end? Girls, ain't no Leo coming to rescue *you*—save yourselves!). Ophelia, another watery maiden, had about as much heroism. Hmmm. . . for years, I've been fooling around with the idea of rewriting *Hamlet* from Ophelia's point-of-view, and having her kick Hamlet's indecisive butt. Both times I directed *Hamlet*, I wished I could cut Ophelia out of the play, because she's so damn passive (Hamlet is wishy-washy, but he at least kills people and keeps the plot moving). At the end of *my* story, Ophelia could learn to swim. So I have a title, *Ophelia Learns to Swim*. . . but what the hell does this bimbo do between Page 1 and the big swim meet? (meet. . . *meating*? Does Ophelia get eaten by sharks? Oy fuckin' *vey*. . . !) In Brian Cox's video *Acting in Shakespeare*, Cox had Tamasin Olivier, as an exercise, play Ophelia as a total bimbo (which made some of the lines make more sense). Jonathan Miller told me Ophelia's two key lines were, "I do not know, my lord, what I should think," and "I think nothing, my lord." Maybe Ophelia is putting on an act, like Hamlet? She's really smart, but it's gotten her nowhere, so she's hung her brain up to dry? I try to marble *Titanic* into my *Ophelia* idea and see if that kick-starts my brain, but months of pulling my hair out produces no storyline.

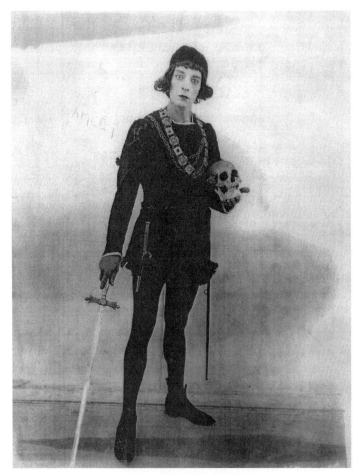

O, heat, dry up my brains!

I decide to try Sundance again. The festival has so many people dying to be volunteers, hoping they might get to chauffeur Nicholas Cage, they now have a competition. Despite busting my hump for the ungrateful bastards two years ago, I am not picked. I start working at Hollywood Video to pay for the trip. It only pays $6.25 an hour, but I get free videos, and I can rifle through customers' files and learn about peoples' tastes.

CHAPTER 24

1998, Age 31

No Dance at Sundance

Miramax puts the dependent back in independent

I used to think that my dentist in L.A. had an incredible memory, because he always asked about the films I was working on six months ago (he asked, and *then* he stuck the drill in my mouth). Then, one time, when he went to fetch my X-rays, I peeked in my file and saw his notes—not about my perfect teeth (*thanks, Mom!*), but about my films. The man was a genius! I went straight home and started my own files about different production companies. I went to the video store, found recent films that I loved, and wrote down the names of the people involved. For Sundance, I make industry flash-cards. I cut bigwigs' headshots from *The Hollywood Reporter* and write their names, occupations, current production companies and film credits.

My Sundance highlight is running into William H. Macy's SUV (lucky for him, I'm a pedestrian, and lucky for me, his SUV is stopped at a light). Parties are now so crowded, you can't hear a thing. There's little talk about the films, but plenty about the deals. "Names" (stars) sell the movies. Indy distributors are "being bought out" by conglomerates (as though they were forced at gunpoint to sell themselves). Miramax is now owned by Disney. A fellow filmmaker tells me to start saving my money for the Sundance Producer's Conference in July—that's where you can actually *talk* to people in the industry. I constantly study my five-inch-thick stack of flashcards, but recognize no one. On the last night, I walk out of a party and pass a man going in—and I *know* he's on my flashcards. He smiles at me. I know I want to talk to him—but who the hell is he? I shuffle through my cards and find him: Mark Ordesky, once a lowly development dude who read *Arch* and wrote the nicest rejection letter I've ever gotten (so nice, he revealed—gasp!—that he had actually *read* my script from beginning to end!). His current occupation? Head of Fine Line Features. I try to sneak back into the party, but no invitation, no three-picture deal, no short skirt, no entrance. Damn! I could stand outside in the snow and wait for Ordesky, but there are four exits, and I can't afford to risk a repeat of the pneumonia of '95. *Rats!* When I get home, I get a job delivering Chinese food to overworked Boeing engineers.

Diet for a New Wroughten Films

Even though *Bill Nye the Science Guy* rejected my sketches, I watch his show on *Nutrition*. When The Science Guy says, "You are what you *ate*—we're made of food!" I almost fall off the sofa. Oh my God . . . no wonder I feel and look like shit—I'm made of partially hydrogenated oils, FD&C Red #40, bleached flour and tap water! I mosey into Elliott Bay Bookstore's Health section, and read the book *Diet for a New America*, by John Robbins (the vegan heir to the Baskin-Robbins Ice Cream fortune). One chapter explains that those conveniently packaged drumsticks were invented not to save you carving time, but because the rest of the poor chicken was riddled with cancerous tumors. I go vegan instantly. When I was a kid, McDonald's was "junk food," so you only ate there once a month. Today, manufacturers of processed foods have managed to stigmatize real foods like beans, grains and vegetables as "health food." I venture into the produce section for the first time in my life and ask people, "What the hell is this and how do you cook it?" The co-op folks kindly help me make vegetable flashcards: "Kale!" "Burdock Root!" "Mustard Greens!" "Potato!" I go off my See Food diet, and remind myself that I can always buy some more food. . . and if I don't have the money, I can always steal food. . . and if I get caught, there's always prison—three meals a day!

I get to thinking (oh, no. . . *somebody stop her!*). . . Female actors are, on the whole, so much better (and let's face it, cheaper!) than male actors, and they're always (rightly) complaining that there are no good roles for them. Maybe I should make a feminist film—a comedy, of course. *Ophelia Learns to Swim* would be perfect, if only I could beat a plot out of this decaying brain. Maybe Mad Cow Disease already has me in its grip.

I want to be who I was at 15 keeps ringing in my head (the devil on my shoulder is apparently napping—maybe he was knocked out by all the omega-3 in my new diet). I want to weigh a fighting weight, have more energy and be strong. At 15, I didn't give a shit what anyone else thought, and I didn't censor my writing—*censor, what for?* What'da mean my idea's "too expensive?" Tyrannosaurus Rex terrorizing my school? *Make him 6" high!* Car crash? *What's the big deal?—get some toy cars, put the camera down low and shoot!* Hell, I would have figured out how to get *camels* (just cut out those little pictures on the cigarette boxes. . . or better yet, talk to the folks at the L.A. Zoo, or Ringling Brothers Circus!). Can I be who I once was, or is it too late?

I should have gone to Butch, not Sundance

I fork over more of Bill Gates's money to attend the Sundance Producer's Conference. In the seminars, I hear a repeat of everything I heard in the $75 IFP seminars. The producers we've paid to mingle with are experts at avoiding wannabes: they excuse themselves to get a better signal on their cell phones and—*poof!*—vanish. Because I'm so low on the rung, I'm not even allowed to stay at the Sundance conference center (is Bob mad at me?). Ten other scumbags and I are shuttle-bussed to a hotel thirty minutes away and miss all the evening parties. I requested vegan meals, but This is Steak Country. I bring my own veggies from the market and, at the table, improvise a steamer out of a strainer and boiling water in a cappuccino mug. After seeing the Executives' raised brows, I realize I should have risked my health so I could appear to be a tough director who, like the boys, can gorge on pizza, drink troughs of Pepsi, smoke cigars and still work a 20-hour day. Well, there goes another $2,500 down the toilet.

Can I have my condo, and eat it, too?

My Grandmother had Katharine Hepburn and Eleanor Roosevelt. Mom had Audrey Hepburn and Jackie Kennedy. I had Jane Fonda and Nancy Reagan. Today, girls have Anna Nicole Smith and Monica Lewinsky. I have lots of energy to invest in *Ophelia*, but she's going under. I can't find any hook, any way to send a few thousand volts through her thick skull. She goes back in the drawer with all my other quarter-baked ideas. More and more no-budget filmmakers are running up their credit cards to make their "feature debuts." If I do it, too, it isn't going to be press-worthy. What worries me is the stories that *aren't* getting written; true-life tales of all those filmmakers who go over the credit card cliffs like lemmings. I wonder how many women filmmakers convince themselves they really love their boyfriends, simply to get a roof over their heads? I want to take a careful, calculated risk. The problem is: if I logically, Spockly, access the downside, I'll never take the leap; the odds against me are too great. But if I'm going to go over the cliff, I want it to be for a film I really love. The script has to be better than *$on for Sail's*.

Omama's second (and last) husband dies, and her lawyer calls me, asking for my social security number so he can send me a check for my share of the inheritance. I have totally forgotten about Omama's promise about putting her money away for me to buy a motor home. Would she mind if I bought something immobile, like a condo? My share is "about $90,000." *Holy Omama!* Okay, *this* is a *sign*: I *have* to make a low-budget film! Can I have a condo, too? Put half down on the condo, and use the other half to shoot a film with one of those new digital cameras? I hope God rewarded Omama with a big Winnebago in the sky. Now, half of whatever cash her second husband didn't take with him is coming my way. I wish I made documentaries; I could make one about me buying a Winnebago and taking off in Omama's place. God knows the *industry* wishes I made documentaries. But I don't like real life—I only like actors. Documentaries are easier for women to break into (because there's no money in it, of course!). Society thinks women should only use their imaginations for decorating the house, and women directors should stick to "human interest" stories. We can only fantasize about being rescued, like Cinderella, or Rose in *Titanic*.

The Return of Rommel

Earlier this year, after reading in a health magazine that hair dye is carcinogenic, I stopped dying my hair black. My hair grows like a weed, so it's all now grown out now. . . and I've gone red again (I was born with black hair, which fell out three months later, and grew in flaming red; then *that* fell out, and I turned into a blonde [but only literally]). My hair is now a darker red, like a fox. . . a sign that it's time to go to war?

New York, Take Three. Unlike Sundance, the IFP Market is not picky about whom they allow to volunteer. At the "Short Films—Getting Noticed" seminar (they should have subtitled it, *"yeah, and good luck!"*), a representative from the Sundance Channel comes to show us the way to fame and feature film fortune: we should send our shorts to the Sundance Channel, where they will be programmed at 2am (when only other short filmmakers are watching) and we will receive $1,000. A filmmaker raises his hand and tactfully points out, "Uh, it costs at least $15,000 to make a 16mm short film, and The Sundance Channel only pays $1,000. . . you see the economic difficulties we're encountering?" The Sundance executive huffs, "Sundance is providing the *best* opportunity for exposure. Frankly, we think filmmakers should *pay* to be on The Sundance Channel!"

Jürgen Vsych. . . the Young Filmmaker who had enough! I'm beginning to understand why their festival and channel was named after a notorious robber. As Mr. Redford is probably too busy to have a chat with his arrogant minions, I take charge. I stand up, give the programmer the middle finger salute and sing out, "FuuuuUUCK YOU!" (Well, it's not exactly Rommel, but it's a start!) The Sundancer has already launched into his next spiel, so I'm not sure he even heard me. . . but everyone on the IFP staff has. I am stripped of my Volunteer Badge. I am also slapped on the back by several fellow filmmakers as I'm escorted out of the building, and avoided by others who don't want the Sundance programmer to see them in the vicinity of this rebel rouser. I have undoubtedly ruined it for future IFP volunteers, who will have to submit to psychiatric evaluations and sign legal documents promising they will not come within a hundred feet of the panelists. Have we just witnessed the grande finale of Jürgen Vsych's career? I decide to think *positively*: no. . . I've just be given more time to spend in the Metropolitan Museum of Art and go to Broadway shows! Bring in da Noise, bring in da Funk!

Dr. Lecktor, I presume. . .

After *da Funk*, I see *Art*, starring Brian Cox. After the Anthony Hopkins incident, do I dare approach another Dr. Lecktor? Well, Cox is the *original*..I don't *think* he's a Method actor. And he's Alan's dad, so how bad could he be? I get past the stage doorman and wait for Cox to say goodbye to his other visitors. Brian vaguely remembers me from the Old Vic. I give him a video of *$on for Sail* and *PYR,B.* He says he'll watch them, and I should come back in two days and we'll have "a nice chat." Brian doesn't get a headache from watching my films: "They were very *idiosyncratic.*" As it's been years since I heard a big long word, I almost snap, "Who are you calling an *idiot*!?" I tell him I'm thinking about moving back to L.A., and he says I can stay in his house there while I apartment-hunt. *It's a sign.* And I have nothing to fear managerial-wise: Brian's manager is Matthew Lesher (who also reps John Vickery—*it's another sign!*). Matthew is scary but never screams, and even though I'm the lowest director on the Hollywood totem pole, he has a soft spot in his little manager's heart for me: John Vickery's big scene in *$on for Sail* has helped John land some big-bucks voice-over gigs. Maybe Matthew will look at me and think, *That woman's short film paid for my entire snow globe collection. . . just think what her next film might do!*

When I return to Seattle, *Sign Number 3* is taped on my door, in the form of a note. *No,* I am not being evicted for not paying my rent; I have never been late paying my rent, not once, I would like to make that clear right here and now to all my future landlords; despite being an Independent Filmmaker with no awards, *and* an ex-musician, I am a financially responsible person who always pays her bills on time. Thank you. What the hell was I talking about?. . . oh, yeah—I'm being evicted so the new owners can turn the apartments into Oakwood Corporate Housing. Of *course*, I can return to my home after they install garbage disposals and dishwashers, but there will be a slight increase in rent. . . from $690 a month to $3,500.

My cut of Omama's estate doesn't arrive by Christmas as promised: Omama's second husbands' third wife's son is suing to get my inheritance, and there will be a delay. . . oh, just a few months, my lawyer assures me. My smart Omama made her second husband's future wife sign a wrought iron-clad pre-nuptial agreement: when he dies, her little angel gets half the money he has left, and *that's* that! So there's nothing to worry about.

I bid farewell to my co-workers at the Chinese restaurant. I'm getting out just in time: Boeing is about to lay off 30,000 workers who will no longer need Chinese delivery. On New Year's Eve, I hit the road, praying I don't crash head-on with a truck in the Anderson Split Pea Soup-thick fog in the San Joaquin Valley.

CHAPTER 25

1999, Age 32

Ophelia Learns to Swim

Dr. Lecktor's Fun House

I make it to Chateau Cox, Brian's house in the Hollywood Hills. When Brian is filming on location (which is 90% of the time), he rents out rooms to various actor friends—and they all smoke. So I move into an apartment with a casting director who needs a non-smoking, non-cat-owning roommate. I wait for Omama's inheritance, so I can go house/condo/motor home shopping. After my lawyer takes his fee, there's not going to be enough left for a place in L.A. . . . Death Valley, maybe.

Bitches in Film

Go to a Women in Film event three years later, and I run into the same middle-aged male attorneys who are still trying to pick up chix in flix. One of the charities WIF patronizes is *Dress for Success*, where producers donate their old Armanis to low-income women (who will end up spending half their salaries on dry cleaning). I ask WIF if I can be on the receiving end; my one decent outfit falls off me because I've lost so much weight (thanks to my macrobiotic diet and swimming). WIF is appalled: "It's not for *members*; if you're a member, we *presume* you can afford Armani!"

I stop payment on my WIF membership check, phone Brian Cox and ask Hannibal Lector #1 if he'll sign my BAFTA application. You're supposed to have two signatures, but I tilt up my nose, waltz into the BAFTA office and announce, "I only have one name. . . but it's *Brian Cox*." They grab my application and assure me it'll be fine. And my check doesn't bounce, so I'm in the door! But only literally. The BAFTA screening committee quickly rejects *PYR,B* and *$fS*. Do I really want to pay dues to yet another organization that refuses to screen my films?

Swedish Suicide, or Ophelia?

Okay, I'm never going to make it in Hollywood, but what else do I love to do? What can I do really *well*, besides write and direct? Uh. . .

The three options: 1) Wait for Omama's money, then buy a condo in Bakersfield, sit in it and rot. 2) Take my credit cards, see Europe, sneak onto Fårö Island and say hi to Ingmar, and then when my cards are maxed out, throw myself into a fjord. 3) Make *Ophelia* (I still have no script. . . but hey, that's never stopped anyone in this town!).

I decide that, for just five days, I'll force myself to sit down from 8am-5pm and work on *Ophelia*. Nothing jells.

On the seventh day, I think, what if Ophelia met the Superheroines and Supervillainesses from my *Almost Live!* sketch?

Ta-da!

I turn off the phone and write *Ophelia*. It's a horrid experience. Unlike my first seven features, I'm not *trying* to write no-budget, I *have* to, or it will be for naught. I have to reject not my first five too-expensive ideas, but the first twenty-five. Eighteen days later, I finish. Despite writing with a financial garrote around my neck, it's funny, it has good roles for women, a witch flying on a broomstick, lots of special effects, scenes involving water, a talking rag doll, and a big fight scene at the end! I couldn't work in a camel, but we have a cat! I sense it's going to cost $110,000; and another $10,000 for film festival publicity. That's excluding two years' rent, food and car expenses I'll accrue while making the film. Because nobody on the crew will really care if I lose my shirt, I draw up a $70,000 budget and pray no one on the film steals my credit cards.

The Producers

Good news: Shirley and my composer/sound designer love the script. Bad news: not enough to work deferred (traditionally, on no-budget films, the D.P., editor, composer, writer, director, producer, and actors are not paid, but get copies of the film for their reels). My composer says, "I have a family to support," and demands $10,000. Shirley doesn't specify an amount; she just keeps repeating that she's "a professional" (she's joined the union). The next day, at an IFP composers mixer, I meet Bronwen Jones, a funny Australian. When she admits her favorite recent soundtrack is Marc Shaiman's *South Park*, I hire her instantly!

I send the script out to my usual hit list, and it's sent back astonishingly fast—"The opening *Titanic* scene alone will cost $1 million—we'd have to build a tank!" I reply, *Tank? We'll shoot it in Dave Fennoy's swimming pool!* The vacant looks. That's what I'm going to do from now on—scare the shit out of fraidy cat producers on Page 1! I see the opening of my next script: "Fade In: Helicopter Shot—Loch Ness. Nessie breeches!. . . "

John Sayles comes to an IFP screening of *Limbo*, shot by Haskell Wexler—a great film. At the Q&A, I ask Sayles what sort of traits I should look for when hiring a D.P.

"*Obedience!*" he replies instantly.

Sayles thinks for a moment of other necessary traits.

He adds, "Obedience!"

Irene Roseen from *$on for Sail*, likewise, won't work for deferred, but she recommends I talk to Ben Guillory at the Robey Theatre Company. I hire Ben to play our Superhero "Testosterone Guy," and Ben recommends a Native American actor named LaVonne Rae Andrews, who I cast as Superheroine "Mother Nature," and LaVonne recommends a production manager who knows a crew willing to work for $50 a day. Matthew Lesher gives me the name of an entertainment lawyer, and recommends several of his former assistants as potential casting directors. To find a new D.P., I advertise: "Women especially encouraged to apply." Several male D.P.s call me and threaten to sue for discrimination. I tell them, "Please do—I would *love* the publicity!" I beg for donations and discounts, and apply for the few grants that still exist in America (I wish someone would nominate me for a MacArthur "Genius" fellowship). Except for brief trips in Seattle elevators, I don't mingle with The Rich and Mighty. None of the people whose houses I clean want to invest in "an unproven artist" (what do they want—*80* short films?!), and when I ask my dentist, he whips out my file and recites his notes about all those visits where I admitted I lost money making films. A wigmaker gives me $400 for my hair (which I was going to chop off for production, anyway). I move into my own $1,000-a-month apartment so I can have a casting facility, production office, and a place to shoot inserts.

My Cinematic Clock Ticketh

There will soon be a strike, or a de facto strike. Both the Writer's Guild and SAG contracts are up in mid-2001, so there will be a huge rush to wrap production before the contract deadlines (*we'll fix it in post!*). It'll be next to impossible to get equipment, crews, or cast. In January, I'll be up against Pilot Season, when actors scurry about from dawn to dusk searching for a series gig (and, hence, lifetime security). I suppose I could wait *until* the strike, and then get everyone *super*-cheap! (Actors would be working illegally, but they'd be well-fed, off the streets and on a soundstage where they belong.) Also, Bronwen, my composer, is going to have a baby in June.

A representative from Coca-Cola phones and asks about product placement (i.e. having Ophelia drink Coke in a scene). I yell *no!* slam the phone down, and then calculate how many toilets I'm going to have to scrub in order to support my crew's Coca-Cola habits. Well, tough! *Ophelia* is not going to accept donations from a company that sells a drink that does nothing but rot teeth. Besides, this may be the last time in my life I'll ever get to stick to my principles. After *Ophelia*, I'll probably be homeless and lucky to get a job directing soft-drink commercials. Well. . . I'm sliding into the gutter with some principles! I write to my favorite environmentally friendly companies: Aubrey Organics, Erewhon Natural Foods Store, Seventh Generation Recycled Paper Products, Glad Rags, Luna Bars and Gabriel Cosmetics. I have a scene in *Ophelia* where the Superheroines acknowledge their sponsors, so we can show their products without bringing the story to a screeching commercialized halt. Of course, the companies whose products I actually use can't afford to give me wads of cash, but they send us free samples.

The Lilian Baylis Prayer

I hire Stephanie Merrick, one of Matthew Lesher's former assistants, as the new casting director (the first one burst into tears when Susan Smith [an agent] yelled at her). Stephanie shares my taste and is good at making the actors feel at ease. I give Stephanie a long wish list of character actors, semi-names and up-and-coming young actors, but they are all "unavailable" (at least for a SAG Experimental film). A name would sure help sell the film, but one star's perks would cost more than the entire film. Lilian Baylis, the evangelical theatrical goddess of the Old Vic Theatre, would fall to her knees in her office before every new production and pray. The night before we start casting sessions, I recite the same prayer:

"Please, God, send me first-class actors. . . *cheap!*"

I'm still nervous about whether or not Ophelia is a character that the audience will stick with for 90 minutes. If I can't find a good Ophelia, I'm not making the film. The first actor Stephanie brings in Julia Lee, one of Lesher's clients. She's a great actor, funny, and easy to work with. Well, that was easy! In fact, she's so terrific, I announce, "We're shooting 35mm!" I've been to Sony and Fotokem's demos of digital vs. film. Digital STINKS; *Super-8* looks better! The only decent digital format right now is Sony's High Definition, which costs a fortune and is full of bugs.

Advice for no-budget filmmakers: write roles for women 18-25 years-old and 60+, and male character actors under 30—*they* can act! Avoid 28-60 year-old males: the decent ones are all employed and supporting their actor wives. Matthew Lesher likes me, but not enough to let me have just one of his middle-aged male clients for two measly days to play Ophelia's Dad ("Brian's not available! Andy Robinson's not available! John Vickery's not available! Ian McNeice's. . . "). The William Morris Agency sends me George Gray's headshot and game show demo reel. George is hysterically funny, and we cast him as Ophelia's horrid brother Larry (get it? Laertes/*Larry*. . . oy vey). We even coop a Coppola—Chris, who works mostly as a director. We cast him as Hamlet (in *Ophelia*, he's an out-of-work hammy actor working as a delivery boy).

I'll give just one example of why no-budget films should never shoot in L.A. (this paragraph could be a whole book): Breakdown Services, the company that lists acting jobs, is free for every studio and big producer in Hollywood—but if you're a flat-broke producer making a film under SAG's Experimental Agreement, they charge you $25.

I comb through the script constantly, playing that game every director dreads: "Where Am I Shooting Myself in the Head?" (when you're writing, it's called "Killing Your Darlings"). First to go is the Broom Witch's cat (I'll try to work her into my next film). To my casting director's great relief, I cut the two eight-year-old characters, Superheroine *Young Lady* and Supervillianess *Daddy's Lil' Princess*.

We'll lose the cool 8-80-year-old age span of the characters, but now we won't have to deal with stage mothers, social workers and on-set tutors. I think the crew should bake me a cake for my artistic sacrifice (getting rid of the children and the animal).

And these two sped westward the glory of a departed sunset

A horse! a horse! my kingdom for a horse!

December 4th: *Ophelia Learns to Swim* begins shooting. So what if Professor's proclamation came true—it didn't take a *decade* for me to direct a feature—it took a decade and a half. *He* still hasn't made a feature, and he's almost 70 years old—*nyah nyah nyah*! I'm used to being the youngest person on the crew—usually by ten years or more—so I'm startled to realize I'm now the oldest person on the crew—by ten years or more. Eeek.

By the end of Day One, it's painfully obvious that our D.P.'s husband is not a gaffer as she claimed, but an electrician in way over his head. He fiddles and fiddles with the lights, and it gets worse and worse, and ends up looking like a t.v. sitcom (over-lit and flat). As Ophelia's house is supposed to be ugly, this is not a catastrophe, but I fear for the upcoming scenes.

The actors are great and energetic. We have no dailies, just weeklies, and only on video: I'll be cutting on an AVID for the first time. Our editor is a woman who worked for *Playboy*, where she spent most of her time cutting around Playmates' implant scars. We shoot with short ends (the studios' leftover film), so the most frequent words heard on this set are the camera crew yelling, "Roll out!" immediately followed by the director yelling, "Oh, *shit*!" The money saved buying short ends doesn't make up for the amount of time we lose during production changing the magazines.

After teaching high school, the world's most frustrating job is being a perfectionist director working on a no-budget film. I'm offering very little money, so people have little motivation to do the work—except for fun, which making a comedy usually is not (there's definitely nothing funny about directing comedy). The costume department decides to pocket their allotment, forgo a trip to the Salvation Army, and have the actors wear their own clothes—but they obviously didn't read the script closely, *and* must have been asleep at the production meeting where I stressed that several costumes were going to wind up at the bottom of a lake, so I end up reimbursing the actors hundreds of dollars. The art department also decides to bypass L'Army d'Salvation and go straight to the prop house; it never occurs to them that the rental deposits on my credit card could mean huge over-limit penalties, and make it impossible to pay the caterer (the most important people on the film!); oh, and they also didn't read the part of the script where that $1,500 rented typewriter gets hurled fifty feet out of the Witch's cottage. A mysteriously large amount of equipment gets "lost" (although I learned my lesson on *Pay Your Rent, Beethoven*, and have a 300-pound guy with a machete guard the raw film stock). Some of the crew try to present me with unbelievably shabby work: because they're not working for their usual fees, they feel they have free reign to do whatever the hell they want—*yeah, it's not the color you wanted, but what have YOU done? Just a bunch of shorts!* So many heads roll in the first week, at night, I dream I'm playing Richard III ("Off with his head! So much for the prop master!").

Bitches on Dollys

The D.P. slows to a tortoise's pace. Even though we start cutting shots, we still fall behind schedule. On Day Three, John Sayles's mantra starts ringing in my ears: I tell the D.P., "*This* is the shot!" then I go to talk to the actors, and come back to find she's moved the camera; she, her husband and the continuity boy (who wants to be a director) have decided on their own that it would be better to do an entirely different scene next. And, of course, they haven't bothered to inform the A.D. or me. As Ophelia's look changes from scene to scene, Julia Lee has to keep going back to makeup (I'm amazed the poor woman has any skin left at the end of the day). The production manager doesn't care about going over schedule (I stupidly agreed to pay him by the day). Breaking in a new D.P. is harder than replacing an actor, but insubordination must be dealt with swiftly. I whip out another credit card, get another cash advance and call Shirley. We pay her a salary way below union scale, but higher than anyone else on the film.

I didn't think things in the camera department could get any worse . . . until Shirley arrives. After a take, she brags, "It was good for ME!" implying the actor (or the director) is a moron if they need another take. When I playfully snap at *her* for blowing a shot three times and needing another take, Shirley explodes, then bitches loudly under her breath all the way through the next take, making sure she's too soft for the sound department to pick it up, but loud enough so *I* can (she then mutters, "What's the matter—can't you focus on your *ack*-tors?!"). Our 1st A.D. is soft-spoken and wants to be liked by everyone. When he gently nudges, "Uh, Shirley, you have five minutes," she yells "Fuck off!" while laughing, sounding like Billy Connolly. Shirley probably thinks she's being lovably tough in an absent-minded kind of way; "I don't wear a watch when I work!" she laughs. The lighting is better, but her focus is always on the wrong actor at the wrong moment, killing punch lines. Now it's obvious to me why Shirley has never shot a comedy. The energy is draining out of the film. At least with D.P. #1, we were getting half our shot list. With Shirley, if we get one shot an hour, it's a miracle. I think Shirley thinks I should just be grateful for her pretty pictures, and it's my fault for not being able to afford a better gaffer and better equipment. Shirley *knows* I've been scrubbing toilets for a decade, I've been working on the script for years, and I have every dime invested in this film—and yet, she doesn't give a damn that we're not making our days. Even if she *is* mad at me for not hiring her in the first place, it's no excuse for squandering my life savings.

For this much money, I should be having *some* fun, but every night before I go to bed, I find myself praying for death.

Millennium Approaches

Shirley's meticulousness grows. We have a 20-hour day, during which we not only don't make the day, we don't even make 1/4 of the day—and we're at our most expensive location, the most remote, and the damned coldest. I feel like forming a union and striking against myself for intolerable working conditions. We can either cut the script (then the plot won't make any sense; there is *no* fat to trim), cut the shot list (which is already so bare bones, it will turn into 100% master shots—*Zzzzzzzzz*. . .), or keep going on this way, and the budget will quadruple.

The one semi-affordable body of water I've found in L.A. County turns out to be too polluted for Ophelia to take her plunge (Shirley yells, "*Rewrite!*"). To top it all off, 'flu takes out the crew one by one. On my 33rd birthday (oh dear. . . this is the same age Jesus snuffed it!), I decide to shut down production for the first time in my career, and start after the New Year (just in time for Pilot Season!). I'm buying time to decide what to do with Shirley. If there's some way to handle this beastie, I can't think of it: if I bark at her, she'll get revenge by slowing down even more, and there goes the film *and* the one friend I have in this world. If I keep going with Shirley, I'll have one beautifully shot yawner. I don't have enough credit cards to pay for the time Shirley needs to get her shots. With the impending strike and rising prices, the budget will soar past $300,000, and that's just to get it in the can. And that's *if* we lose no actors during Pilot Season. If Miramax or Lion's Gate like the film, their accounting department will order a copy of my credit report and know that I am in such a desperate position, I'll take anything—meaning *nothing*, no advance. All scenarios lead to the same ending: Bankruptcy. Goodbye apartment, hello Honda Accord! Will I even *want* to be Shirley's friend after that? (Maybe she'll have so many great shots for her reel, she'll let me sleep in her tool shed.) An undone movie is worthless. At any cost, I must avoid joining all the other beached films. I've never shelved a film, and Julia Lee is great, and she and *Ophelia* deserves an audience. Omama's money—if it ever comes—won't even cover half the debts I've already run up. I vowed years ago *never* to get into debt. . . but Michelle Kwan's family sure did. They even had to sell their house and move in with her grandparents. Susan B. Anthony got into debt when her feminist newspaper failed. Do they still send people to debtors prison? (More material! And prison looks *great* on an author's resume!)

Christmas. I write the lyrics for a song that might be good for
Ophelia's end credits. . .

A long time ago, like sixteen hundred years.
Before t.v. and computer engineers
A woman in Alexandria
Dressed just like Princess Leia
And no matter what, she always perseveres
Hypatia, she really rocks
A sweet nice girl, dumb like a fox!
She thinks the thought and walks the walk
She even sings like J.S. Bach!
She's good at math and science stuff
A pretty chick, but she's no duff
She studied hard, she used her head
When guys made fun, she said "drop dead,
I'm trying to work, you stupid putz!"
She's smart and brave—I love her guts!
The men chased her for her good looks
But she always carried her own books
"I'd like to be dined, bejeweled and pearled
But I'm too busy changing the world!"
Hypatia! she really rules
Stands up tall, fights her own duels
She kicks butt, suffers no fools
Hypatia, man, she really rules!
She's someone all the men want to get
But to their chagrin, she's a bachelorette
"I'd love to date, be flattered and girled—
But I'm too busy changing the world!".
She was a pagan—not fashionable
Her enemy, Archbishop Cyril
He told his gang, "Go get that lass
Hunt her down—and kick her ass!"
They tore off her clothes right there and then

With abalone shells, they flayed off her skin
Burned her bones, and then her books
They laughed and jeered, "So much for her looks!"
The seeds are there, the earth is hoed
We reap the harvest you once sowed
Not much has changed since you died
We know you fought, we know you tried
We will, too. . .
We remember you. . . .
Thanks, Hypatia!

Julia Lee as Ophelia. . . waiting for the director to fill the pool

CHAPTER 26

2000, Age 33

Spock to the Rescue!

Lauren Birkell as the Broom Witch
(the broom is being re-strawed)

The Wroughten Apple

Where's the Y2K mass meltdown of the world's computer systems that I was so looking forward to? (It would have been a great excuse to pull the plug on *Ophelia*.)

Walt Disney went bankrupt halfway through making his *Alice* cartoon. He obviously didn't have a Visa card. Thanks to Visa, *I* can keep going. I must finish the film, to show people I'm committed (or should be committed).

The production manager is thrilled that the lab and telecine bills have plummeted since Shirley came aboard. No matter how many ways I explain it to the jackass, he can't comprehend it's because hardly any film has run through Shirley's camera.

Fire my best friend?

I call Shirley and tell her we have to pick up the pace; *at least* three set-ups an hour. She snorts, "Do you want one good shot, or three bad ones?"

I reply, "Actually, I want *ten* 'bad' ones—the comedy is flying out the window!"

"That's *your* department, babe—I just set up the camera!"

I don't care if she is my elder; she has no right to talk to me like that. What the hell is the matter with her? Every time I've asked why she's taking so long to light, she sings that song D.P. #1 loved to sing: "I'm doing this for *you*, so *your* movie will look good." The truth is, Shirley believes my ship sank when I didn't hire her initially; why not salvage something in the wreckage for herself? She can get a lot of great shots for her reel, make a little cash, and have a blast openly bad-mouthing the director to the crew and within my earshot. She knows all my weak spots, especially that I won't fire her.

The devil sitting on my shoulder gets a Vulcan nerve pinch on *his* shoulder, and is knocked off his perch. Spock then parks himself gently on my dislocated shoulder and says in his low-key tone, "It is not logical to continue with Shirley."

The new guy on my shoulder
(so that's where *Ophelia's* cat went!)

194

As a writer, I must play the game "Kill Your Darlings"; as a director, "Where am I Shooting Myself in the Head?" As a Producer, it's "Find the Rotten Apple and Toss It." My eyes must drop millstones, when fools' eyes drop tears. I call the production manager, tell him I'm letting Shirley go, and unless he finds a new D.P. by tomorrow, I'm taking the last $500 of credit on my Alaska Airlines Visa and flying to Hawaii (possibly ending with a swan dive into a volcano). The production manager says he's heard of a D.P. named Cricket Peters (our 2nd A.D. Alexa "Squirrel" Motley is a gem—why not try another animal?). The production manager tells Shirley the news before I can call her myself. Shirley phones me, all cheery and making inquires about my health, before chiming, "Just out of *curiosity*, when were you going to tell me I've been fired?" Her final words to me *("Good luck!")* ring in my ears (I wish she'd just said, *"Drop dead!"*).

Cricket-o-Vision!

Cricket introduces herself to the crew: "Hi—I'm D.P. *du jour!*" and gets thrown into the fire on her first day; we've lost Chris Coppola (he was only available during December), and my beautifully choreographed Big Fight Climax goes to pot when three actors show up and inform me they have to leave in an hour to go on auditions for paying jobs (Pilot Season!). One actor fails to show up at all. I have to re-write on the set, and my perfectly-woven subplots go flying out the window. I wanted to show that a woman director could stage a great battle, but all I've got in the can is a cutesie, bitchy fight.

Despite the chaos, I'm actually more relaxed—what a luxury it is, having a D.P. who follows directions! I don't have to worry about where on earth Cricket will move the camera when I turn my back to talk to the actors! A D.P. who says "No problem!" when I say "You've got ten minutes to light this and get two takes!"—and then *does it*. A D.P. who merely smiles and makes a tiny *hmmm* when I show her the skateboard dolly she has to use because D.P.s #1 & 2 in fifteen days of shooting put us seven days behind schedule, so no Fisher Dolly for thee, D.P. #3. I love Cricket! Could this be the beginning of a beautiful friendship? Hell, *no*, because I'm never going to get close to anyone in this business EVER AGAIN! They're all a bunch of piranhas who will dump me when I go broke and only are acting chummy because they want to be my guests at BAFTA screenings!

We edit all our footage and Bronwen starts writing the score, but we still need two more days of shooting (ten would be better: then Cricket could reshoot *everything* D.P.s #1 and 2 shot). I cancel my cable t.v. and subscription to *The Hollywood Reporter*. I call L.L. Bean and Land's End catalogs and beg them to take me off their mailing lists (*Lead me not into temptation*). Video rentals, auf Wiedersehen.

Ophelia Swims!

Two months and two new credit cards later, I find a new "brook" for Ophelia to swim across for the finale (actually, a small Sparklets drinking water reservoir in Lancaster). The water is sparkling clean and a lot warmer than Dave Fennoy's unheated swimming pool, so I can throw Julia Lee in longer and not feel too guilty. Shooting is finally *fun*. With a smaller, obedient crew, Cricket and I pop off shots, and I even have time to eat lunch. We go back to the expensive witch's cottage, and wrap on April 1st (no fooling)! I lay in some of Bronwen's music, send videos to film festivals, and pray for more credit card offers so I can finish post-production.

I find a CGI animator to do the shots of the witch flying across the moon. The technical incompatibilities of transferring the digital animation to film drag on for months, so we can't lock picture. Then there's another two-month delay when Bronwen has to stop working to give birth (what a lame excuse!). I'm worried about Bronwen's health, and her mind. Will her brain go straight into the diaper pail? Our sound designer can't wait any longer and he takes a paying job. I feel like I'll be working on *Ophelia* the rest of my life.

Hi ho, hi ho, it's off to Work I go

I get rejected by every finishing fund, and all the money I had set aside for publicity is long gone. I can't afford to go to a festival even if the festival flies me over. I can't get a full-time job to start paying off the bills because I'm sitting around waiting for people to have free time so they can afford to work on *Ophelia*. I find a job with flexible hours: Refusal Converter for the Census, convincing aging anti-government hippies to fill out their long questionnaires. Compared to getting your no-budget crew to cooperate, it's a piece of cake—and I get paid $14 an hour! Working for the government, I at last understand the phrase *going postal*: the stupid redundant paperwork, the incredible inefficiency, the redundant paperwork, the forced unpaid overtime (did I mention the stupid paperwork?).

Omama's money finally comes. After my lawyer takes his fee, my inheritance, which was supposed to be $90,000, is $27,215. My credit card balances are so high, I can't even think about them without getting dizzy. If I pay only the monthly minimum due, it will take 67 years to pay them off (it's a good thing the average life expectancy of the women in my family is 110—I'll be able to relax and enjoy the last decade of my life!). I spend an hour every day organizing my bills, making grafts and charts and calendars to keep track of payments, making balance transfers (always searching for those 3-months @ 2.99% interest offers), and calculating how much more than the minimum payment can I afford to pay. I was planning to move out of my apartment after one year, but rents have skyrocketed, so it's actually cheaper to stay put. I may have to sell my umlaut for food.

When the Census ends, I sink even lower: into telemarketing, selling theatre subscriptions to lonely old people, working alongside women who are serving community service for acts of road rage. I sign up with four temp agencies and ask them to please not send me to any entertainment companies, lest someone in the industry should see me. Great. God entrusted me with this exquisite brain, and I'm using it to telemarket and make photocopies. What a waste. Mrs. Vincent was *wrong*; I should have learned a lucrative trade—like quantum cosmology—so I could make some decent money between films and keep my brain exercised. I need a profession. I hate every job, except writing and directing films, but I would rather telemarket than create crap. My macrobiotic diet, walking and swimming are helping my arthritis. . . could I be a musician again? My shoulders are still dislocated, so cello is out.

I finally get smart and start calling film festival directors, telling them how many films I've made (i.e. mine is less likely to suck than most), how I'll publicize like mad, pack the house—and if they waive the fee, I'll send them a video. Ten festivals agree (I get rejected by them anyway, but I save $500!). Not one of the women's film festivals will waive the entry fees. Because I pity my fellow females, I send them the fee, but I'm rejected by every one. I can't understand why any womens' festival would reject *Ophelia*. I have no idea what this industry wants. I only know what *people* (civilians) like me will like. Frankly, my dear, I'd rather watch *Romy and Michelle's High School Reunion* than most Best Picture Oscar winners. All I want from a film is good acting, a witty script, decent visuals and sound, and not too many boom shadows.

Oh, my babies. . . !

With her bouncing baby boy in the crook of her arm, Bronwen finishes the *Ophelia* score and does a great, great job. I find a sound editor who—I discover too late—is more interested in going out on his boat than in sound editing. He cancels sessions every day the boaters report is favorable (I'm used to being at the mercy of the weather, but never in *post*-production). Serves me right for hiring a guy who could afford a boat; someone working out of their garage would be more motivated and interested.

John Gielgud dies. *Rats! Rats! Rats!* Now I'll never get to remember how nice he was to me outside the Old Vic.

Spock to the Rescue!

Alec Guinness also dies. At his BAFTA memorial, I meet Guy Green, the D.P. of *Great Expectations* and director of *A Patch of Blue*, and Ronnie Neame, the director of *The Horse's Mouth*, *The Odessa File*, and the best bagpipe movie ever made, *Tunes of Glory!*

A few days later, I see an advertisement for a free bagpipe concert (Free, Good!). *These* pipers are terrific, and I learn that pipes sound great if played well, but if not... *bleccch!* That's why I didn't like the photo-op piper in Edin—

I could play pipes! You don't have to lift your arm very high to squeeze the bag, so it would hurt—but not kill—my shoulder!

... but, no, I can't afford lessons, or the time to practice, I'll never become good enough to play in public, my landlord will kill me if I practice at home, pipes cost $1,500... and that's *all* I need: playing an instrument whose main audience would be drunks in pubs, drunks at Highland Games, drunks on the street. I sit in my room for three weeks waiting for my sound editor's boat to develop barnacles, and the only thing I can hear is a wee voice chanting, "I want to be a piper! I want to be a piper!" (I don't *think* it's Spock. Is it my devil? He's been awfully quiet lately.)

I start bagpipe lessons the day before my 34th birthday. My "logic": for my next film, I can play them to mesmerize the cops when they try to shut us down for filming without a permit.

"Permit?"

CHAPTER 27

2001, Age 34

The Woman
Feature Director

A Director's Work is Never Done

Our sound "designer" says he's not "tinkering" anymore with *Ophelia*, even though we're missing forty-four cues ("The film sounds good to ME!"). I foolishly paid him his third and final payment on the day he was supposed to finish work—but before he actually finished work—so he's got me by the ends of my DA88 tape.

I pay for the optical soundtrack and watch the answerprint of *Ophelia*. In addition to the missing cues, the last scene is out of sync. I sit there gripping the armrests, thinking, "This is *it*? And there were so many details that could have improved the film—nothing three thousand dollars couldn't have fixed. . . !" I have to let work on the film go, and keep chanting, "I did the best I could with the money I had; I'll make another one. . . " *Ophelia* is four and a half times longer than *$on for Sail*, has four times as many locations and a cast five times bigger, and it was shot seven inflationary years later—and yet, it only cost twice as much. My next feature should look and sound *great*! I'm a feature director!

At a BAFTA party, I ask Guy Green if he'll watch *Ophelia Learns to Swim* and give me his opinion. Unlike the seventy-five previous celebrities who beamed, "Yes, *of course* I'll watch your film—I *so* look forward to seeing it!" Mr. Green actually watches it, returns my video (rewound, no less!), and he writes, "I think your film is technically very good." Guy won an Oscar for shooting David Lean's *Great Expectations* (starring Alec!), so maybe I should frame that!

This Guy thought my film was "technically very good"!

Maybe it's just that Mr. Green has seen so many badly-shot student films, a little focus impresses him. *I'm* disappointed with the technical aspects of the film. I wanted to show that I had the right stuff: I'm no "chick director" scared of technique; not only can I coax actors out of their trailers and give them some sort of motivation to say all those lines, but I'm a great shooter, too—Ridley Scott with a low six-figure budget! The irony is, I wanted to get into features to do deeper characterizations (something I didn't have time to explore in shorts). But in *Ophelia*, I couldn't afford to do it, either. It takes a decent amount of screen time and very experienced actors to execute a full-blown character.

Time to Sell. There's only one way *Ophelia* will get any attention: Being in A Big Film Festival, like Sundance (they've already rejected us), Toronto, or heck, even Temecula Valley (it's now HUGE, and less than two hours from L.A.). And, for really independent filmmakers, it's next to impossible to even get into those festivals—they're now being used as premieres for multimillion-dollar films that already have distributors.

I spend my days entering festivals and learning bagpipes. As pipes have three drones, not two, I practice calling them a "set," not "pair" of pipes (remember, High School Drop-Outs have difficulty counting all the way up to three). God, they're hard to blow. Good thing all my neighbors have 9-5 jobs; I feel free to make horrific deafening noises. I practice for hours, building up my lip like a weight-lifter until the muscles in my lips twitch and drool soaks the front of my shirt.

Bronwen's husband, who works at RAND (Research and [No] Development), recommends me for a short-term job. In the middle of RAND training, I get an idea for a film—a bagpipe movie! *The world's first bagpipe musical!* Oh, great, I get my first decent-paying job, and *now* my brain decides to kick into high gear. But Wroughten Films must strike while the iron is hot. After *Ophelia*, I promised that I was gonna scare the shit out of fraidy cat producers on Page 1...

Page 1

Distributor and production company's logos. Scottish Regimental Drumroll over "A Wroughten Film," and "The Bagpipers."

EXT. LOCH NESS—MORNING

FLYING over mountains surrounding the loch.

MUSIC: "Nessie's Set"

DISSOLVE TO:

Skimming above the water toward Urquhart Castle. As we reach the shore, tilt up to reveal a man playing small pipes sitting on a rock near the shore. He's about 40 and wears hiking boots and a corduroy shirt.

DISSOLVE TO:

The Loch Ness Monster. Nessie's head and long neck, like an elegant periscope, serenely glide through the water, resembling the famous "Surgeon's Photo." But this, of course, is no fake.

DISSOLVE TO:

From 200 feet offshore, WIDE ANGLE of the Piper and Urquhart Castle. Nessie swims into the corner of the frame, heading towards the Piper.

CU PIPER

He sees Nessie. No reaction—this happens all the time.

MS NESSIE

Nessie heads straight towards the Piper.

THE PIPER

a very weird expression grows on his face. He keeps playing, but he's now focused on the shore.

THE SHORE

Nessie is coming out of the water.

THE PIPER

She's never come out before!

NESSIE

waddles onto the shore. She looks like a relative of the plesiosaurus—a brontosaurus with flippers.

TWO SHOT FROM SIDE

The Piper is 6 feet tall. Nessie is 6 inches tall.
[why, she must be a cousin of Tyrannosaurus Tex!]

The Piper looks down at Nessie and smiles benevolently. He may be Scotland's most recognizable symbol, but this is his country's biggest tourist attraction.

Nessie looks up, bears her sharp teeth and licks her chops.

The Piper double takes.

Nessie slowly starts shuffling towards the Piper.

THE PIPER

stops playing.

NESSIE

keeps waddling full steam ahead.

ECU PIPER, then

FAST TRACK BACK

Revealing the Piper now wearing full Highland dress and holding the Great Highland Bagpipe. He fires up.

Nessie does a double take.

The Piper plays at Nessie, moving toward her, saying musically; "Bite me? I'll kick your ass!"

Nessie shuffles backwards, scared out of her wits.

When it's clear the Piper has subdued the Monster, he continues playing for his own enjoyment.

And when it's clear all the Piper wants to do is dance, Nessie starts bobbing her head in tempo to the piping.

The Piper looks at her encouragingly.

Nessie starts jiving, lifting her flippers up and down.

The Piper and Nessie dance together.

CUT TO:

INT. BOARDROOM, THOUSANDS OF MILES FROM
SCOTLAND—DAY

ECU ROB

waking up. Rob is 39, baggy-eyed. He's fallen asleep in a staff meeting.

                        C.E.O.
        —in the next fiscal quarter we can project a
        loss of three percent at the current rate, and. . .

Flustered, Rob nods his head in agreement with his boss and starts playing
with the tape dispenser.

Rob looks across the table at his best friend, JOHN, 39, who likewise is
having difficulty staying awake. John looks at Rob quizzically.

Rob turns the tape dispenser around and points to the word "Scotch."

John's eyes light up.

INT. ROB'S LIVING ROOM—NIGHT

Rob pours Scotch for John and himself. . .

(Are ye trembling in yer wellies, *fraidy cats?!!*)
  I write *The Bagpipers*, feature script #9, in six and a half days—a
new Rommel Record! I could have done it in three days if I wasn't
working full-time. It's the culmination of everything I'm good at—
music, comedy, drama, and male characterizations. And yes, I even
got the Broom Witch's cat into the script! That would be great if I
could do this for all my future scripts—just goof around for a few
months, exploring a subject I love, then BANG!—a screenplay ef-
fortlessly pops out. Watch for upcoming Wroughten Films featuring
Beethoven (got the script already!), dinosaurs (oh dear—$), killer
whales ($$), cats ($$$!), skeletons, swordplay, figure skating, archery,

karate, gregorian chants, tafel music, Scotland, Ireland, magnificent death scenes, World War II—and camels, Camels, CAMELS!

John Sayles, Woody Allen, Ingmar Bergman, Pedro Almodovar and Ang Lee get praised for their strong women characters. For *The Bagpipers*, *I'm* going to get slaughtered for making a film about four men, where the women are just wives and girlfriends. I'll never get praise for my male characters—just the usual, "Why isn't the lead *female*?!"

Mike Kerrigan, a journalist I meet at a BAFTA screening, likes *Ophelia*. He used to be on the board of the Temecula Valley Film Festival. A few months later, *Ophelia* gets into the Temecula Valley Film Festival (what a surprise! Well, it's about time these coincidences applied to *me*). Time to sell, sell, sell!

Rommel's Front

The *Los Angeles Times* tells me, "We already did story on a woman director" (five weeks ago—we must be over our quota for the year). I point out that they do at least one story a week on new male directors. Vacant silence. I waste time and money trying to get press in L.A. I should have hired a "front"—some nebbish-looking guy to pretend *he's* Jürgen Vsych. He would get a *L.A. Times* article, reviews in the trades, and praise for creating such vivid female characters.

On September 5th, sitting in Baja Fresh, eating my Burrito Mexicano hold the meat, I have An Epiphany: *I will never work another office job again!* Is it a sign that I'm going to get a nice big advance for *Ophelia*? I've also had the same dream every night this week: two small airplanes, one right after the other, fly into a window in the apartment tower across from me, and the tower explodes.

On the morning of September 10th, I see flames shooting out of the apartment tower across from me. Luckily, I was wrong about the planes—it was just a chicken left overnight in the oven.

Time to Pay the Piper

On the morning of September 11th, three days before the World Premiere of *Ophelia Learns to Swim*, an article about me and *Ophelia* appears on the front page of the Arts section of the *Press-Enterprise*: "Pipes, Loans, Hair Finance Film" with a cool photo of me with my pipes, wearing my handmade *Ophelia Learns to Swim* T-shirt. I decide to skip my morning walk so I can answer all the "Congratu*lations*!" phone calls from those people who always come crawling out of the woodwork every time my name appears in print (agents, mostly). . . but the phone never rings.

I drive to Charlie Chan Printing to photocopy press kits, and get there in record time—I don't pass a single moving vehicle, just dozens of people sitting in their cars staring straight ahead like zombies. There was no space shuttle launch or re-entry today that could have gone awry. . . Charlie Chan, normally packed, is empty. "Haven't you heard?" Four planes bound for L.A. crashed, thousands of people killed—and terrorists are probably flying over L.A. right this minute! I call my temp agencies for that day's assignment. They scoff and say to forget about working today, or tomorrow, or ever: "This will put us out of business; go back to scrubbing toilets!" Jo Moulton at the Temecula festival calls, asking if I'm still coming—of course! But the *Ophelia* cast and crew pull out. I've seen World War II newsreels, so *I* know what to do—Hollywood must spring into action! It's time to entertain the troops (and civilians)!

It quickly becomes apparent I'm the only person in Hollywood who feels this way. Since Hollywood (and the rest of America) is completely shut down, I take my bagpipes and go to the park to practice *Rhythmic Fingerwork*. As I play, people come over, open my closed pipe case and put in dollar bills! A few ask me to play *Amazing Grace*. More people come running over and ask me to play it again. I open my case, and make enough money to go to the movies, *and* Baja Fresh! People want me to keep playing, even though my lips go numb. WOW! And I was just practicing taorluaths and D-throws; just imagine how much dough I'd make if I could play *Scotland the Brave*. Hey, I think I've found a profession!

The Temecula Valley Film Festival is an unmitigated disaster. People in L.A. won't drive down ("I don't think it's an *appropriate* time to be having a festival"), and most of the celebrity honorees flake out— only Ray Charles is enough of a trooper to brave the terrorists who are no doubt plotting to hijack hot-air balloons and bomb the Pechanga Indian Reservation's casino. Of the *Ophelia* gang, only Cricket and Julia Lee's mom come. 65 of the 100 people who come to my screenings are guys age 18-25 (Hollywood's target audience!)— and THEY LIKE IT! God, why can't people in the industry see this?! I meet a fellow woman director who has a great documentary in the festival, and we go to Starbucks after our screenings. Is there any sight sadder than two women directors weeping into their herbal teas? At least *she* just married a man with a job, so she can afford to go on the festival circuit. This was my only shot.

Death by Chocolate for The Chocolate Fox

For $37, I get a performance permit for Santa Monica's Third Street Promenade. I can only play for ten minutes before I start making elephant noises and the spit starts flying, but I earn about a dollar a minute (if only it were physically possible to play for five hundred minutes a day!).

For $800, I rent the Chaplin Theatre at Raleigh Studios for a November 7th industry screening, and spend three weeks calling, faxing and emailing every person in Hollywood. *God, please let me meet people who love the film, get a distribution deal, and get a job out of it.* The morning of the screening, I have Another Epiphany: the screening is going to be a total wash-out. I've had lots of RSVPs, but I know none of them are going to come. It's too late to get a refund from Raleigh, and I've bought way too much Trader Joes' chocolate.

Ten minutes before the screening, people finally start arriving. I take one look at the middle-aged guy Paramount Classics has sent, and I know he's going to hate *Ophelia*. He's only here to avoid spending an evening with his family. The other guests are an idiotic D-Boy and D-Girl from a small production company I've never heard of; the Irish band *Craicmore*; a few civilian friends; and two agents who rejected *Curl Up and Dye* (christ, if they rejected *that* script, why bother showing up?). Of the cast and crew, only Hamlet (Kristofer McNeeley) shows.

Terry "Dad" Gilliam was right—you *can* judge the audience reaction solely by the backs of their heads. I've never seen a film from the back of the theatre (fifth-row aisle is my favorite seat. You can almost leap into the movie from there), but I need to see the heads. The audience is silent, but attentive. Not until our chain-smoking, Armani-wearing villainess Virginia Svelte appears and bonks the audience over the head do they get that it's okay to laugh. During the best scene in the film, where Ophelia's drowned mother comes to give Ophelia a wake-up call, the Paramount Classics guy's neck tenses. Oh, shit. . .

Scene 35. INT. BEDROOM—NIGHT

Ophelia sleeps. A "drip-drip" sound. Ophelia opens her eyes. A 40-year-old woman is sitting at the foot of the bed, dripping wet, seaweed in her hair, sand on her face.

OPHELIA
Are you Virginia Woolf? I'm not afraid of you!

WOMAN
Why do you think I'm Virginia Woolf?

OPHELIA
'Cause you're all wet! You've been swimming in
your clothes! Don't you have a bikini? Boys like
girls in bikinis. . . Virginia Woolf drowned herself. She shouldn't have done that. She was

useful. She was a good writer! So what if she went mad occasionally. That's okay, as long as the dishes get done. Are you Natalie Wood? Oh, I know! Are you Mary Wollstonecraft? She tried to drown herself, but she didn't succeed. A man rescued her. She died giving birth, but her daughter wrote *Frankenstein*, so that's okay.

WOMAN

I'm your mother.

OPHELIA

(pause)

I haven't written anything. . . is that okay? Hamilton will rescue me. Well. Am I talking too much? Dad calls me the babbling brook. Hey, cheer up!—better smile so Dad will love me. Did you want to say something?

MOTHER

Wake up, darling.

OPHELIA

Have I been asleep?

MOTHER

Wake up.

Scene 36. INT. BEDROOM—MORNING

ECU OPHELIA'S EYES, popping open.

OPHELIA

Oh!

Ophelia is in bed. Pull back to reveal Dad and Larry kneeling by the bed, concerned.

OPHELIA

Dad! Larry! I was dreaming. I was kidnaped by
a witch, and Mother Nature was there, and
Handyman, and Virginia Svelte. . . !

DAD

(pats her hand)
Well, we're glad to have you back. . .

Ophelia beams, relieved it was all only a dream.

DAD

. . . because there are fifteen loads of laundry to
be done!

Ophelia double takes.

LARRY

And this is my room now!

Larry grabs the edge of the mattress, lifts it up, and Ophelia rolls off the
bed and splats on the floor. Pull back to reveal the room now decorated by
Larry's things.

DAD

That witch won't be back to take my pickup
truck, will she?
(to Larry)
We'd better get a car alarm, just to be sure. . .

Dad and Larry leave. On the floor, Ophelia is really awake now!

Two scenes later, the Paramount Guy starts squirming. Well, that's
an interesting sensation, watching four years' work and your entire
life savings go down in flames. My dream of being one of the few
women to make a second feature right on the heels of the first and
not wait another seven years—*poof!*

Having decided against using booze to staunch the flow out of the building (if they don't want to talk to me sober, let 'em go, says I), all the industry people immediately vanish. A bagpipe buddy, *Craicmore*, and my boss from RAND like the film. David Bell, an artist who worked at RAND with me, says he'll recommend me for a medical survey job next year. So, I got one thing I prayed for: a job (it's a job in the field, not in an office, so I guess my Epiphany was right). Damn it! I should have specified "*directing* job!"

Follow-up time. Miramax claims they sent someone to my screening, and "We passed." I know the name of every person who has seen the film so far (all 160 of them), and no video tapes are floating around. I wish I had the nerve to yell, "You weren't there! Why are you lying, you sacks of. . ." Maybe they'd respect that! (Some companies only want directors who play hardball.) Or did Miramax and Paramount Classics huddle together, pick the Paramount guy as the sucker who has to sit through yet another independent film, and have him report back?

I call everyone and ask, would they like to see a video, since they couldn't make the screening? (There was nothing else going on in town that night, except more news footage from 9/11.) I'm dead in the water. . . why don't I just say, "Hi, I didn't get any offers!"? I keep calling, hoping that someone, just *one* person, won't ask the dreaded "Who's in it?" (I've tried quipping, "A bunch of terrific theatre actors you've never heard of!" but that only gets vacant silence.) I spend $500 making VHS copies. Post-9/11, with all the new security, it's impossible to sneak onto studio lots or drop by production companies (everyone thinks they're so important and influential, terrorists will target *them*). Everyone is also using 9/11 as an excuse to postpone or cancel doing things they don't want to do ("Due to the *national crisis*. . .").

It's Walt Disney's 100th Birthday. I'm now 35, middle-aged (provided I make it to 65 like Walt did). I get another maid job. The Rich and Mighty are making do without butlers and resort to having their maids open their front doors (the *shame!*). For Christmas, I storyboard *The Bagpipers*, and build up my lip enough to busk for two hours a night. Unfortunately, I make less than $1 a minute, and less than that if it rains, and less still if the Lucky Brand Jeans store manager comes out, yells at me and scares away my audience—and if the Hari Krishnas park themselves within a hundred feet of me, *fuggeddit*. After "I've never seen a *lady* piper before!" and "Can you play *Amazing Grace?*" the most common thing people say, when putting money in my case, is, "You have red hair!" as though it were an accomplishment. Might as well put the hair to use; no more cutting off my biggest marketing tool to pay the rent.

CHAPTER 28

2002, Age 35

The Lady Piper
From Hell

Brian Cox hires me to play pipes at his Near Year's party. His young actor girlfriend Nicole is eight months' pregnant (goody—more Coxs to direct!). I ask John Allan, my bagpipe teacher, if he wore a kilt when he used to busk. He says, "Of course—you *don't*? NEVER PLAY BAGPIPES IN PUBLIC WITHOUT WEARING A KILT! You'll get gigs!" I find a $6 kilt in a thrift shop, and unofficially join the Stewarts (well, I *did* win the Princes Trust). That night, I get hired to play my first wedding! My directing career has been great training for playing at weddings: I'm used to being stoic while the people around me run around with their heads half off. Funerals are a lot more fun (for a piper, anyway), and I get to hang out in grave-yards, with the trees and flowers. And busking is good training for directing: holding my ground when enraged people try to make me move; getting dirty looks and things thrown at me and still staying on the tune; posing for photos; and remaining Buster Keatonesque when I get catcalls like, "*Hey, what's under your kilt?*" and "*Transvestite!*" (I was the only girl to wear slacks in nursery school, so I feel I've come full-circle.) For the best-paying gigs, most people, alas, want the traditional big fat guy piper: they call me to ask, "Do you know any MALE pipers?" (I naïvely reply, "Uh, gee, no—can *men* play the pipes?") Every funeral I get is for a woman, or for a man who "would have wanted a woman piper," or else I'm hired by a vengeful female relative who wants me to literally pipe on the grave of the dead sexist pig. Still, it's the first paying job I've ever had that doesn't make me want to slit my throat. I must be the only person in the world whose day job is being a musician!

A woman from a distribution company phones, asks what rights are available for *Ophelia Learns to Swim*, and says, ". . . we'd like to acquire it." As I haven't heard this phrase in years, it takes a moment to sink in. Her company is at the bottom of my choices for distribu-tors; they mostly handle thrillers, soft porn and horror. I call the director of a film similar in tone to mine and ask him if liked the way the company distributed his film. He says he's not seen a dime from them, even though his film sold to The Movie Channel and Australian t.v. The company estimates my film will do $200,000 in sales over two years (notice they didn't say, ". . . will make *you* $200,000. . . ") I agonize for several weeks. Acquiring *Ophelia* will cost *them* nothing (the days when distributors gave advances are long gone), but it will cost me lawyer fees and "deliverables" (music and effects tracks, 35mm slides, trailers, video transfers, etc.). I could easily sink another $10,000 into credit card debt and not have a single sale, just the ability to say, "I have a distributor" (one that no one has heard of). It's the same situation I was in two decades ago with sub-standard agents. I decide to sign. The company doesn't take me out to dinner, or lunch, or even offer me coffee (gee, even *I* serve tea and cookies—and I let my guests use as many tea bags as they want!).

A caterer calls me on the morning of St. Patrick's Day and asks if I can play pipes for a film crew's dinner tonight, and it's not a very big-budget film, so will I give him a good deal? It turns out the film is Steven Spielberg's *Catch Me If You Can*! They're shooting at the old Boeing hanger in Downey. I'm nervous—one little squeal of the chanter could destroy my chances of ever working at Dreamworks! For better or worse, I'm ignored by the crew (and glared at by D.P. Janusz Kaminski, although his dog loves the pipes [most dogs do]). The only other person I recognize is the bad, *bad* guy (and dancer!) Christopher Walken. I guess Steven, Leo and Tom are being privately entertained by The Chieftains.

I'm a director. . .
but what I *really* want to do is PIPE!

One of my housecleaning clients invites her friends to come over and watch their maid, who is going to Cannes next week, kneel on their bathroom floor and scrub their toilet. *Ha ha ha! Wait, wait— let's get a picture of this!* Much as I love entertaining and making people laugh, the maid is tired of this kind of humiliation, and announces she's retiring from domestic service to descend into the humiliating existence of a street performer. Now that I'm freed from scrubbing pots and pans, my finger technique improves.

I had a miserable experience last time at Cannes. . . but now I have a distributor, and a *feature*. As I hate festivals and markets but love bagpipes, I decide to not do my usual round of fax/email/calls to the usual suspects, and instead spend the time mastering *Le Marseilles* and *The Can-Can* (*Cannes Cannes?*) so I can play them on the Croisset next to a poster of *Ophelia*. At least two thousand journalists take photos of me, but only Italian tourists give me cash. I have a sign in my case reading, "My feature film *Ophelia Learns to Swim* is being distributed by. . . " I should have made signs that read, "Did you know that donations can be written off as a business expense?" and "Did you know that if you take a photo of a piper and don't give them a tip, you will die a horrible, horrible death?" A few journalists later tell me, "I thought about giving you a tip." Well, it may be the thought that counts, but alas, my landlord does not accept thoughts. Ironically, my best money-making tune in France is *The Battle of Waterloo*. The unavoidable clouds of cigarette smoke give me bronchitis and put an end to my busking after only three days. My distributor fails to make a single *Ophelia* sale—and no wonder: they "forgot" to have any screenings, the poster they designed looks cheesy, and the flyers look like they were made on a broken color copier. All the other films they rep have four-color glossy flyers. I blew five years of accumulated Alaska Airlines credit card miles this trip, miles I was saving to go to the World Pipe Band Championships in Glasgow.

Maybe I shouldn't feel so bad. Theatrical distribution is becoming rare for non-blockbusters. Even a great film like *The Golden Bowl*, a Merchant-Ivory film with Nick Nolte and Uma Thurman (christ, how many names do you need?!), got dumped by Miramax and was given a tiny theatrical release by Lion's Gate. Must *every* screen in America show *Spider-Man* and *Attack of the Clones*?

Tyrannosaurus Tex Goes Home

Ophelia gets into the Fort Worth Film Festival, even though Mike Price, the festival director, doesn't know who the hell I am; *he just liked the film!* Mike is a literate, Truman Capotesque guy with great taste (note inclusion of *Ophelia*). *Tyrannosaurus Tex* would go over well here. . . a pity it no longer exists. The filmmakers' goodie bags have coupons for pizza and Jamba Juice—no fucking shampoo! Now *this* a man who knows how to look after his poor, hungry filmmakers! Ten years to the day after the World Premiere of *Pay Your Rent, Beethoven*, the *Fort Worth Star-Telegram* prints a great article about how I made *Ophelia*, and includes the photo Cricket took of me in my shopping cart dolly. About thirty middle-aged couples who read the article come to my 7:30pm Saturday night screening. The festival is held at the AMC multiplex in Sundance Square (Sundance! Is there *no* escape!?). There's another "independent" film playing in the theatre next door: *My Big Fat Greek Wedding* (which cost "only" $5 million). *Ophelia* is shot better than that film, and has a better script and a better leading lady. This is the first time one of my films has played in the middle of America (Fort Worth may be "Where the West Begins," but these folks are *Southerners*, they inform me). The Fort Worthians laugh LOUD. A few people who bought tickets for *My Big Fat Greek Wedding* accidentally walk into *Ophelia*'s screening—and they stay! TEXANS like *Ophelia* (not exactly a Republican film). I have a future! The Real-Live American movie-going public enjoys my work! God, I should have videotaped the backs of these heads—I could have shown it to the Studios as proof! Mike Price presents me with a special award he whipped up at the last minute: "Best Marketing." I hope Hollywood realizes it means I got the most butts in seats!

Catch Spielberg, *If You Can*

BAFTA is having a screening of *Catch Me If You Can*, with a Q&A afterwards with. . . *drumroll.* . . Spielberg! I'm going to see him in the flesh for the first time (I don't really count the Hollywood Bowl in 1982). As BAFTA screenings are open to any sleazeball with $10, they sternly announce beforehand, "We are a PROFESSIONAL organization, and approaching guests with scripts and autograph books is prohibited." But they didn't mention VIDEOS. And I *did* kinda work on his film (piping for the troops!). BAFTA has started to whisk their Q&A guests away before anyone can even say hello. Before the screening, I write to BAFTA to complain: "Why can't young filmmakers meet guests for a few minutes? Why let autograph seekers and big-eyelashed bimbos ruin it for everyone? And why do those free BAFTA memberships always get raffled off to the richest members? How 'bout giving some free memberships to members who are unemployed? And why the hell is there never tea or cucumber sandwiches at the receptions?!"

We Concur!

I love *Catch Me if You Can*. Peter Morris, the moderator, lets me ask the first question (I only get to ask Spielberg *one* question?!). I ask Spielberg how he and John Williams chose to use vibraphone in the very funky score, and his eyes light up, "You liked that? Me, too!" and he speaks to me just like two directors shooting the breeze. Needless to say, the usual aggressive crowd surrounds him afterwards, then he's whisked away.

Kevin Spacey's Trigger Street Productions announces that they want "unique material," so I send them *The Bagpipers*. His D-Girl responds, "Uh, not THAT unique! More straight genre stuff that will appeal to the studios." The D-Girls keep telling me I'm too "wacky" and my work "isn't broad enough" and my films will appeal to "no one" except *them*, because *they're* brilliant!

Little Old Lady Piper from Pasadena
(she's the terror of Colorado Boulevard!)

Christmas—I have too many credit cards to pay off, so I have no time to write. I play pipes in Old Town Saturn (Pasadena) in front of The Crate and Barrel (God bless them, they never call the cops on me). Retail business is slow, and people dump pennies, not dollar bills, in my piper's kitty. I make half the money I did last Christmas, even though I'm playing four times better. New Year's Eve is very lucrative: Rose Bowl fans flood Pasadena, and the Washington Cougars' fans tip *big*. Oklahoman fans don't tip at all. GO, COUGARS!

CHAPTER 29

2003, Age 36

Director Barbie

Show me the Kwan!

The Washington Cougars lose the Rose Bowl. Okies celebrate by hurling paint at me, ruining my Royal Stewart kilt.

New Year's Resolutions:

1. Stop Being Crazy. By crazy, I mean doing the same thing over and over again and expecting different results (e.g. wasting time and money sending videos to production companies, agents and film festivals, and believing they'll actually watch them).

2. Only to Do Fun Things (within economic reason). To hell with "taking the right steps"! No more begging phone calls. Only go to movies I really want to see, not because I might meet someone at the screening who could help my career.

3. Throw out all those Plan B's and C's, and focus all my attention on *The Bagpipers*. Don't waste another minute wondering how I will advertise for maid jobs when inflation makes those $1 bagpiping tips worthless.

4. Spend more money on things vital for my career (reference books, a website, new glasses, a digital camera, dumbbells. . .), and go back into debt, if I have to (Michelle Kwan would still be skating in a shopping mall if her family didn't spend the money necessary to get her to the next level). If I keep going on the way

I have in the past, my tombstone will read: "Here lies Jürgen Vsych. . . only made one feature, but paid all her bills on time!"

(sung to the tune of "What Would Brian Boitano Do?"*)*
What would Michelle Kwan do
If she were me today?
I'm sure she'd spend a buck or two
'cause that's what Michelle Kwan would do!

Other people must have made the resolution *Learn to Play the Bagpipes*, because in January, I suddenly get a dozen students. Most drop out after they discover they'll actually have to *practice*, but I get three steady students. I've never taught before, but I must do an okay job; they come back for more torture the following week.

The UCLA Archives screens Dorothy Arzner's films (Jodie Foster helped pay for their restoration). Arzner's women characters are victims of their times and circumstances, but they're not whiny or weepy, and they wise up fast. Too bad Arzner never wrote her autobiography. . . maybe I should write *mine*, while I'm in a foxhole preparing to charge. That way, there'll be three books young women directors can read (Alice Guy Blaché and Leni Riefenstahl wrote their memoirs long after their careers ended).

I drop by a toy store to see what kids are playing with these days. There's a fancy Lego set called *Studios* that comes with Lego crew members, a real digital camera, and editing software. It's endorsed by Steven Spielberg. The Lego director has a beard, and the Lego cameraman has a mustache. The Lego girl on the crew gets to be the clapper/loader. Young girls are going to see this, and wonder years later why they never dreamed of being a director. I like Dreamworks's logo—a little boy sitting on the moon fishing. But when *I* work for Dreamworks, the logo is going to be a little girl (and she ain't gonna be CLEANING the stupid fish, neither!).

Michelle Kwan, the Olympic gold medal "loser," has taken over from Tara Lipinski as the endorser for *Figure Skater Barbie*. There's a new line of dolls: Barbie® the "indie film producer looking to cast her leading man. . . she is secretly in love with Ken® the Art Director." The package describes how she interviews Ken® for her new project and "desperately tries to ask pertinent questions, but finds herself continually lost in those soulful pools of blue, all the while thinking, 'This man has it all.'" (". . . except a decent portfolio!" Give me a bucket. . . I'm gonna throw up. . .) Barbie® The Producer has waist-length bright orange hair, 4" high heels, a bare midriff and half-closed eyelids. There's also Simone™ the makeup artist, and Melody, the blue-haired production assistant who is so inconsequential, she doesn't even need to be copyrighted. Of course, there's no *director* Barbie. . . wait! I have a new goal: I should be the one to endorse *Director Barbie*!

The Woman Director

Wroughten Films
White Honda Accord Parked on 3rd Street
Los Angeles, California
November 14, 2003

Dear Mattel,
Please manufacture "Director Barbie." It should be part of your "I Can Be. . . " Career Series, and not the higher-priced Collector Edition series (there are already too many directors from wealthy families; let's give poor girls a chance to dream big!).

The Specs:

Clothes: broad-rimmed hat, jacket, loose-fitting trousers with pockets and low-heeled shoes

Accessories: eyeglasses (never trust a director who doesn't have myopia!), storyboards and director's chair with "Barbie" written on the back.

Hair: should be a human color and shorter than waist-length (directors don't have time to deal with that much hair), and include ponytail holder; Women Directors are sensible creatures who keep their hair out of their eyes and do not drive other people crazy by non-stop grooming and hair-flipping!

Eyes: should be wide-open and big but not vacant, and easy on the eye shadow. Smile should be subtle and convey thoughtfulness and intelligence, not mindless glee at simply being allowed on the set.
I do not even need to mention that the chest size and leg length should be of vaguely human proportions, do I?

Friends forever!
Jürgen Vsych
The Woman Director

P.S. When my film *The Bagpipers* is released, we could do a movie tie-in: *Bagpiping Barbie*! Just picture red-haired Barbie in a Tam O'Shanter, jabot blouse, kilt, kilt hose and ghillie brogues, with her pipes (*Barbie¨* written on the bag cover, of course), and her wee pal Nessie the plesiosaur. I bet it'd sell more than the bagpipe-toting "Fat Bastard" action figure from *Austin Powers*!

Hollywood Ending (please God, let it)

I've been very lucky. Lots of girls don't even have a library card. For me, respect means getting the same salary as a man. In many parts of the world, it means not being raped or set on fire by your father-in-law.

A lot of my dreams have come true. I got to live in Scotland and play bagpipes (though not at the same time), I got to fly a lot (as a passenger. . . at least I never had to serve booze to people!), and I've made 29 films. I never *got* to make my first feature: I paid for every dime of it myself. And I made my films without being anyone's daughter, wife, sister, girlfriend, cousin, niece, or in-law. I never had to bat a single eyelash to make my films.

Wes Anderson flopped with *Bottle Rocket*, yet he still got financing for *Rushmore*. After *that* flopped, he got to make *The Royal Tennenbaums*. Alexander Payne's *Citizen Ruth* and *Election* weren't hits, but he still got financing for *About Schmidt*. M. Night Shyamalan's first two films didn't do well. Francis Ford Coppola's first *three* films bombed. After *Ophelia Learns to Swim*, how will I get the financing for *The Bagpipers*? Will I have to sell my children (*Curl up and Dye* and *Pay Your Rent, Beethoven*) to pay my rent?

It's hard not to be bitter. What if Danny Kwan (Michelle's dad) was my dad? I would have been the best and most famous woman director ever by now! What if I'd be born a man? (God, don't even go there. . .) What if I'd had more food as a kid? My brain would work better, and I'd be 6 feet tall! What if. . . ?

I wonder where I'll go next—Scotland? Canada? Ireland? New Zealand? (I never met a Kiwi I didn't like!) Australia? Texas? France? (25% of French films are directed by women—*mon dieu!*) Who likes the bagpipes? Mexican families always give me good money when I busk. . . Thanks to *The Bagpipers*, I'll eventually get to go back to Scotland, and *I shall return* a feature director (and a piper!).

Castle Vsych

A big dream of mine is to have *wroughten* be in the dictionary, like *Pythonesque* or *Capraesque*. Maybe, someday, I will be an adjective (*That movie was very Vsych*).

I also want my own museum: The Jürgen Vsych Castle (it can be a smallish one). It will have displays of my old props, Omama's Super-8 Bell & Howell camera, Mr. Nickolas's splicer, and my iMac (visitors in the year 2103 will chuckle, *Only 256 megs of RAM? Oh ho ho. . .*). There'll be a reasonably-priced vegan café, a ballroom converted into a skating rink, and the gift shop will sell the soundtracks from my films and DVDs (or whatever format they've invented for future home viewing). Most of all, I want schoolchildren to watch my films on the big screen in my parlor, and pose for holograms next to the statue of The Woman Director in Her Shopping Cart Dolly. How I wish I could live long enough to hear the boys scoff on the way home, "*I* don't want to be a director—that's *womens' work!*"

Books that influenced me

Directed by Dorothy Arzner by Judith Mayne

The Memoirs of Alice Guy Blaché

Thinking in Pictures: The Making of the Movie "Matewan" by John Sayles

The Magic Lantern by Ingmar Bergman

Close Encounters of the Third Kind Diary by Bob Balaban

Me: Stories of My Life by Katharine Hepburn

Jurgen, A Comedy of Justice by James Branch Cabell

They Don't Get it, Do They? Communication in the Workplace—Closing the Gap Between Women and Men by Kathleen Kelley Reardon, Ph.D.

The Winning Attitude! What it Takes to be a Champion by Michelle Kwan

The Right Stuff by Tom Wolfe

The Ralph Nader Reader

Zen and the Art of Writing by Ray Bradbury (yes. . . I gave him a chocolate bar!)

To order more copies of
The Woman Director, visit

www.TheWomanDirector.com

Audio books, DVDs and VHS tapes are also available.